The Heart of a

Conqueror

RANDALL J. BREWER

CONTENTS

THE HEART OF A CONQUEROR

INTRODUCTION

The story of the children of Israel entering the Promised Land is far more than an ancient historical account - it is a living blueprint for those who desire to walk in victory, purpose, and faith. In "The Heart of A Conqueror," we will explore the timeless lessons embedded in the book of Joshua, lessons that guide us to cultivate the courage, wisdom, and perseverance necessary to step into the destiny God has prepared.

The journey begins at the banks of the Jordan River. For forty years, a generation wandered in the wilderness, learning dependence on God, enduring trials, and watching the promises of God remain just out of reach. Now, a new generation, led by Joshua, stands on the edge of possibility. The first lesson emerges clearly: preparation precedes possession. Joshua did not stumble into the Promised Land unprepared; he was trained, mentored by Moses, and disciplined in obedience to God. Likewise, before we can inherit the promises God has for our lives, we must cultivate a heart prepared for victory - faithful, patient, and ready to act when the moment comes.

Crossing the Jordan River itself was a miracle of faith and obedience. The waters stopped flowing, and God made a way where there seemed to be none. Here, we see the second lesson: God's power is made perfect in our obedience. Conquest is never won by human might alone; it is secured when we align our steps with God's instructions, trusting His timing and methods even when they defy logic or convention.

Then came the fall of Jericho, the first of many formidable obstacles. A fortified city, seemingly impregnable, fell not through conventional warfare but through steadfast faith and disciplined action. The Israelites marched, trumpets blew, and walls crumbled. This teaches us the third lesson: victory often requires patience, persistence, and bold faith in God's plan. We may face situations in life that appear unassailable, but the same God who brought down Jericho can overcome our obstacles if we respond in faith rather than fear.

As the land was divided among the tribes of Israel, we encounter another critical lesson: inheritance demands responsibility and courage. Each portion of the land carried unique challenges and blessings, requiring the people to take ownership and steward what God had given them. Conquering is not merely about claiming victory; it is about walking in the authority and responsibility that come with it. True conquerors do not take lightly the resources, opportunities, or territories entrusted to them - they protect, cultivate, and expand them with wisdom and diligence.

Throughout their journey, the Israelites faced distractions, doubts, and temptations to compromise. Yet Joshua's unwavering faith and courageous leadership remind us of another vital principle: a conqueror's heart refuses compromise and fear. The call to victory demands a life of steadfastness, a refusal to settle for anything less than what God has promised, and a commitment to act with integrity even in the face of opposition.

Finally, the story of Israel in Joshua reminds us that conquest is never just about outward victories - it is about transformation. The Promised Land represents not only territory but the fulfillment of God's promises and the fruit of obedience and faith. Every challenge faced, every wall that fell, and every portion of land inherited points to a deeper truth: the greatest conquest is the mastery of the heart through faith and trust in God.

This book is an invitation to develop such a heart - a heart that rises in courage when fear threatens to paralyze, a heart that trusts God when circumstances seem impossible, a heart that perseveres when the journey feels long and the enemy strong. The lessons of Joshua are not distant history; they are a living roadmap to a life of victory.

As you read "The Heart Of A Conqueror," allow these stories and principles to speak into your own life. May you discover the courage to face your personal Jerichos, the wisdom to navigate your Jordan Rivers, and the faith to walk boldly into the inheritance God has promised you. Step forward, rise up, and embrace the heart of a conqueror - the heart that God designed to overcome, to endure, and to triumph.

| 1 |

"THE LAND OF BLESSING"

In the Old Testament, God called Joshua to lead the people of Israel into the Promised Land. Crossing over the Jordan River was more than a physical journey for the Israelites - it was a spiritual threshold that would usher into their lives a new normal, a new experience of God's blessings. It marked the end of wandering, the closing of one chapter, and the beginning of a new life filled with God's promises. As they stepped into the land flowing with milk and honey, they were stepping into a fresh experience of God's abundant blessings. This crossing reminds us that God often calls us to leave the familiar behind - our old ways, our doubts, our limitations - and step into the fullness of His promises. Just as the waters of the Jordan parted to make a way, God makes a way for us to enter into His best. The "new normal" isn't just about circumstances changing; it's about our lives being transformed by His faithfulness, provision, and presence.

You also have your own personal Promised Land that God wants you to cross over into. When you cross over into what

God has prepared for you, expect a new experience of favor, peace, and abundance. The land flowing with milk and honey isn't just a promise of comfort - it's a promise of life lived in alignment with God's purpose, where His blessings become your everyday reality. Sad to say, most people visit the land of blessing, but God wants you to live there. It is God's desire to lead you into His abundant blessings. He wants to take you to places you've never been before. He wants to take you from glory to glory. Living in the land of blessing is not automatic and it's not accidental. The key to taking new territory, to experiencing a new normal, is to be strong and courageous. God wants all men and women to have courage because courage gives you the heart of a conqueror. It takes courage to step forward in faith and embrace the new normal that God is ready to give.

Ambrose Redmoon said, "Courage is not the absence of fear, but rather the judgment that something else is more important." Courage is doing what you are afraid to do. There can be no courage unless you are scared. It is courage that allows you to rise when challenges loom large, when the path seems uncertain, and when the storms of life threaten to overwhelm you. Courage gives you the strength to step forward despite fear, to keep moving when the way is hard, and to accomplish great things even in the face of obstacles and indescribable hardships that seem insurmountable. Courage is the key that unlocks your God-given potential for it is what allows you to rise to the challenge. Remember, it is not the absence of difficulty that defines your journey, but the courage to press on through it. With God as your guide, courage empowers you to transform trials into triumphs and hardships into testimonies. Rise boldly, for courage is the spark that ignites the extraordinary within you.

Know with certainty that God does not call His children to live in fear or to shrink back when challenges arise. He does not want you to be a coward, timid, or paralyzed by doubt. Webster's Dictionary describes a "coward" as 'one who shows disgraceful fear or timidity in the face of danger and difficulty.' A coward shrinks back in fear when difficulties come. Fear is not God's plan for you. He wants you to stand bold and fearless, to be strong and courageous. From the moment He calls you, His desire is for you to stand firm, to rise above fear, and to walk boldly in the path He has prepared for you. He wants you to be brave and valiant when trials arise because He wants to work in you and through you. Stu Weber said, "The calling of every man is to offer stability to a world of chaos." Strength and courage are not optional - they are a reflection of faith in action. When you face trials, remember that God equips you with His Spirit, His wisdom, and His promises.

In the heart of every man of God is the longing to be courageous, to be bold, to have the guts to do what needs to be done. This longing is not accidental. It is woven into your spiritual DNA by the One who called you, formed you, and equipped you. God never intended His children to live small, silent, or timid lives. He placed within you the fire of His Spirit - a fire that refuses to settle, refuses to shrink back, and refuses to accept less than the fullness of His purpose. Courage gives you the power and strength to never give up. It is not the absence of fear; it is the presence of God in the midst of fear. Boldness is not natural confidence; it is supernatural strength that flows from knowing who walks with you. And the "guts" to do what must be done is not human stubbornness; it is divine conviction - heaven's backbone planted in an earthly vessel. At the core of true Christianity resides courage. It's what causes you to become the man God created you to be despite whatever obstacles you face in the world.

There is a holy courage within you - placed there by the hands of God Himself. Before you ever faced a challenge, before you ever met resistance, before you ever felt fear, God had already deposited strength, boldness, and divine bravery inside your spirit. Courage is not something you have to go out and find; it is something you allow to rise. The person who succeeds is not the one who holds back, fearing failure, nor the one who never fails, but rather the one who moves on despite failure. The Father has already equipped you. The fire is already in your heart. The boldness is already in your spirit. The confidence is already in your identity as His child. Now He gently invites you to let it shine. You are a child of the King and you were made to step into places others avoid. You carry a courage that does not come from this world. So rise up and lean into that holy boldness. Do the hard thing, say the needed word, take the step that feels bigger than you.

God understands our human limitations. What He desires is that when we do fail, we remain firm in our resolve to trust Him. He is never surprised by our struggles, our weaknesses, or the moments when our strength runs out. What blesses His heart is not perfection, but perseverance. When we stumble, He does not turn away - He invites us to stand again. When we fall short, He does not condemn - He calls us to trust Him more deeply. God's desire is not that we never fail, but that failure never causes us to abandon our faith. He wants you to get back up and keep moving forward, not with a tentative, halting attitude, but with a strength and courage that flows from your confidence in Him. When your strength wavers, when victory seems lost, anchor your resolve in Him. When your courage falters, cling to His unfailing grace. Let every setback become an opportunity to declare, "Lord, I still trust You." The person who keeps trusting is the one who discovers the power of God made perfect in human frailty.

God calls you to courageously set aside your fears, your insecurities, your selfishness and sin, and step up and fulfill the responsibilities He has given you. What are the responsibilities of a godly man? Robert Lewis said, "A real man rejects passivity, accepts responsibility, leads courageously, and expects God's greater reward." It takes courage to do all these things. No matter where you are in life, God calls you to do your duty as a man. A real man is active in fulfilling his God-given responsibilities. Taking the initiative to do so is at the heart of every conqueror. Like Joshua, a real man passionately assumes responsibility for his family and the assignment God has given him. Real men seize the moment and take action knowing that, at its core, passivity is cowardice. It keeps a man stuck when God is opening a door. It keeps his voice silent when God is urging him to speak. It keeps his hands idle when

God is calling him to build, to lead, to love, to fight for what is right.

No man wants to be labeled a coward. The world today needs men who are willing to be the tough, courageous men God designed them to be. Deep within every man is the God-given desire to stand strong, to rise to the challenge, and to live with purpose. But in a world that constantly pulls men toward compromise, comfort, and fear, courage has become rare and desperately needed. Winston Churchill said, "There comes into the life of every man a task for which he and he alone is uniquely suited. What a shame if that moment finds him either unwilling or unprepared for that which would become his finest hour." The world today doesn't need passive men. It doesn't need men who shrink back when pressure rises. It needs courageous men - men who refuse to bow to fear, who refuse to let culture define their identity, and who refuse to silence the voice of God within them. Press into the battle and be prepared to shine when presented with what could be your finest hour.

God never designed men to be timid. He placed strength in your spirit, fire in your heart, and conviction in your soul. Courage isn't the absence of fear - it's the decision to obey God in spite of it. It's standing firm when others retreat. It's choosing righteousness when the world celebrates compromise. It's protecting your home, leading your family, defending truth, and walking boldly in the calling God has placed on your life. This generation is crying out for men who will rise up - men who will be tough when life gets hard, steadfast when storms hit, and faithful when the enemy attacks. Men who will carry the presence of God with boldness and refuse to apologize for being who God created them to be. Brother, God has called you to be courageous. Step into that calling. Stand tall. Be the man He designed you to be - strong in spirit, firm in faith, fearless in purpose. The world is waiting for men of courage. Rise up and be that man so they have to wait no longer.

God wants to lead you into your own personal Promised Land. It is there that you'll have a new experience of God's presence, His power, His working, His leading. You'll have a new intimacy of God's presence that you've never had before. To get there you have to have the heart of a conqueror and the strength of a warrior for taking new territory always begins in the heart. Before your feet ever step into new ground, your spirit must rise with strength and courage. You need to "be strong in the Lord and in the power of His might" (Eph. 6:10). To take new territory, you must carry the heart of a conqueror - a heart that refuses to settle, refuses to fear, and refuses to let yesterday define tomorrow. A conqueror's heart is not loud, aggressive, or boastful. It is steady. Confident. Anchored in God's presence. It is a heart that looks at the giants and says, "My God is greater." It is a heart that sees the walls and says, "God will bring them down." It is a heart that knows new territory is not won by comfort, but by courage.

When you allow God to strengthen your inner man - when you choose faith over fear, obedience over hesitation, and purpose over excuses - you step into a new normal shaped by heaven rather than by your past. Your thinking changes. Your expectations rise. Your spirit wakes up to the reality that you were created not to survive, but to conquer. Stand strong and stir up the warrior within you because taking new territory isn't about having perfect conditions or waiting for everything to line up. It's about being strong in the Lord, bold in your faith, and confident that if God called you to it, He has already equipped you for it. Being strong and courageous makes it possible for you to experience things you wouldn't normally experience. Every act of courage becomes a key that unlocks a new dimension of God's favor. Every step of strength becomes a doorway to deeper relationship, unexpected opportunities, and divine encounters arranged by His hand. Fear keeps you where you are. Courage carries you where God wants you to be.

If the people of Israel have to be strong, then Joshua their leader will first have to be strong. Moses said to Joshua in Deut. 31:7,8, "Be strong and courageous, for you shall go with this people into the land the Lord has sworn to their fathers to give them. And the Lord, He is the one who goes before you. He will be with you; He will not leave you nor forsake you; do not fear nor be dismayed." The call to be strong and courageous is based on the absolute certainty of God's presence in your life. Jesus said in Matt. 28:20, "I am with you always even to the end of the age." Rom. 8:31 says, "If God is for us, who can be against us?" There is an enemy out there who roams about like a roaring lion seeking whom he may devour (1 Peter 5:8). There are giants in the Promised Land and you must face them and defeat them in order to experience the abundance of

God in your life. To help you overcome those giants, God has promised you His enduring presence.

God told Joshua, "As I was with Moses, so I will be with you. I will not leave you nor forsake you" (Josh. 1:5). He then said, "Be strong and courageous" (vs. 8). Why? "Because I am with you." God's presence makes all the difference in the world. When you trust in Him, He'll give you the Holy Spirit who will be in you and with you forever. To be strong and courageous, to have the heart of a conqueror, you've got to believe what God has promised. In Gen. 12, God promised Abraham that He was going to give him and his ancestors a land that flowed with milk and honey. He then told Joshua, "Every place that the sole of your foot will tread upon I have given you, as I said to Moses" (Josh. 1:3). God was saying, "The land is there for the taking. Believe Me and go take it." Today, your Promised Land is a Spirit-filled life. It's a picture of a life with the Lord that is experienced to the fullest measure. Jesus said in John 10:10, "The thief comes only to steal, kill, and destroy; I came that they might have life, and have it more abundantly."

Eph. 1:3 says God "has blessed us with every spiritual blessing in the heavenly places in Christ." God has promised you a life of victory and abundance, a life flowing with milk and honey. Those who believe that and are courageous enough to act on that, are the ones who live an abundant life on the earth. This means you'll experience a life filled with love, joy, peace, longsuffering, kindness, goodness, faithfulness, gentleness, and self-control (Gal. 5:22,23). You believe what God has promised, you must now obey what He has commanded. Josh.

1:7 says, "Only be strong and courageous, that you may observe to do according to all the law which Moses My servant commanded you." God's commands are not suggestions to be weighed, debated, or set aside until they fit our convenience. They are holy instructions - life-giving, protective, and purposeful - meant to be obeyed. When the Lord speaks, He is not offering opinions; He is revealing the pathway to blessing, strength, and spiritual victory.

He didn't give us the Ten Suggestions; He gave us the Ten Commandments. They were written in stone by the finger of God. Obedience is not about restriction - it is about alignment. Every command of God positions you to walk in His wisdom, His covering, and His favor. When we treat His Word as optional, we drift. But when we honor His Word as final, we stand firm, unshaken, and victorious. God's commands flow from His heart of love. He knows what you do not know, sees what you cannot see, and leads you where you could never go on your own. Obedience is your "yes" to His perfect plan; it is your declaration that His way is higher, His truth is sure, and His authority is absolute. Choose to obey - not partially, not reluctantly, but fully and willingly. He's God! He's the King of kings and Lord of lords. He has the right to tell you what to do. Every act of obedience unlocks a blessing, strengthens our faith, and draws you closer to the One who commands only what is best for you.

God told Joshua to obey all - not some, all - that the law of Moses told him to do. Jesus asked in Luke 6:46, "But why do you call Me 'Lord, Lord,' and do not the things which I say?" There is a two-word response to the commands of God. Those words are, "Yes, Lord." John 13:17 says, "If you know these things, blessed are you if you do them." Also, feeding on the Word of God makes you strong and courageous. Josh. 1:8 says, "This Book of the Law shall not depart from your mouth, but you shall meditate in it day and night." The Word of God needs to be in your mouth for it is food for your soul. The Word of God is likened to bread. Jesus taught us to pray, "Give us this day our daily bread" (Matt. 6:11). The Word of God is likened to milk. 1 Peter 2:2 says, "As newborn babes, desire the pure milk of the word, that you may grow thereby." The Word of God is likened to meat. Heb. 5:14 says, "But strong meat belongs to them that are mature." God's Word is bread, milk, and meat. It's food for your soul.

Jer. 15:16 says, "Your words were found and I ate them." Think the Word! Talk the Word! Do the Word! Believe what God has promised. Faith begins where trust in God's character is rooted. His promises are not guesses or possibilities - they are guarantees backed by the integrity of the Almighty. When you believe His promises, fear loses its voice and hope becomes your anchor. Obey what God has commanded. God's commands aren't suggestions or optional guidelines. They are divine instructions designed to lead us into blessing, protection, and purpose. Obedience opens the door for God's power to operate in your life. When you walk in His ways, you walk in His strength. Study what God has written. The Word of God is your foundation. It is your light, your wisdom, your weapon, and your comfort. The more you fill your heart with Scripture, the more clearly you hear God's voice and recognize His will.

A Bible that is open consistently shapes a life that is strong and courageous continually.

| 2 |

"GUIDANCE AND PROVISION"

God wants to lead you into your own personal Promised Land, a land where a new normal takes place. Yes, there are giants there and many battles will have to be fought. Thankfully, God will be by your side every step of the way. We don't always know what the future holds, but we do know who holds the future. Life has a way of reminding us that we're not in control. Plans shift, circumstances change, and the road ahead can feel like a fog-covered path. There are moments when the unknown looms large, and fear whispers that we are unprepared for what lies ahead. But in those very moments, God invites us to rest - not in what we can see, but in Who He is. Your confidence isn't built on clarity of circumstances; it's built on the character of God. He is the One who stood at the beginning of time and will stand unchanged at the end of it. Nothing surprises Him. Nothing overwhelms Him. Nothing is beyond His reach or outside His wisdom. When you don't know what tomorrow may bring, your God already stands in your tomorrows.

As God leads you into the future, He'll help you take new territory by giving you divine guidance and provision. He knows who you are, where you are, and what you need. Every challenge you face, every decision you make, is met with His divine guidance. He knows your heart, your purpose, and your needs even before you do. You don't have to figure everything out on your own; He provides exactly what you need at the right time. Trust that as you follow Him, doors will open, obstacles will be removed, and new opportunities will align with His plan for your life. Step forward with faith, knowing that God goes before you, equips you, and secures your victory in every territory He calls you to claim. Psalm 23 reminds us of these realities in a very powerful way. David writes this psalm to give us insight into how God works in our life. He wants to give you confidence that you serve a God who provides your every need.

What does God provide? First and foremost, God provides relationship. You are never alone for God is always with you. Ps. 23:1 says, "The Lord is my shepherd." Make this personal. God wants to have a long and lasting relationship with you. He is your Shepherd and He cares for you personally and intimately, guiding you through every valley and leading you to places of peace and abundance. His care is personal and intimate. He knows your heart, your fears, your hopes, and even the thoughts you keep hidden. In His presence, you are never alone. His love is steadfast, His guidance unfailing, and His desire is for you to walk with Him daily, growing in trust, understanding, and peace. Open your heart to Him today and experience the joy of a relationship where you are fully known, fully loved, and fully cared for by the One who created you. He is not a distant God; He is your constant companion, your protector, and your friend for life.

A true shepherd never walks away from his flock. His eyes are always watching, his ears always listening, and his heart always tuned to their needs. Day or night, in the open fields or the hidden valleys, the shepherd remains nearby. His presence brings peace. His guidance brings safety. His love brings strength. This is the heart of our Lord toward us. He is constantly present in your life. There is never a moment in time when He's not there. He does not abandon us when the path grows dark. He does not forget us when dangers rise. He does not tire of walking beside us. Instead, He cares for us continuously - tending our wounds, leading us to rest, and restoring our souls. If you believe that, you'll boldly move forward not knowing and not caring what the future holds. The word "LORD" in this verse means "Yahweh." This is the fearsome and awesome and holy name of God. He is the ever-present great "I AM." He is your shepherd now and forevermore and He is with you always.

Next, God provides resources. David wrote, "The Lord is my shepherd; I shall not want." This means you shall not lack any good thing. Whatever you need, God will provide. Phil. 4:19 says, "And my God shall supply all your need according to His riches in glory by Christ Jesus." The Message Bible says, "You can be sure that God will take care of everything you need, His generosity exceeding even yours in the glory that pours from Jesus." David wasn't just speaking of green pastures and still waters - he was declaring a promise that God Himself is your provider. Whatever you face today - whether a need of the body, the mind, or the spirit - remember that the same Shepherd who guided David, who comforted him in trials, is guiding you. Trust that He sees your needs, anticipates your desires, and provides according to His perfect timing. When God is your shepherd, you will never truly lack; He equips, sustains, and enriches every area of your life.

Sheep cannot care for themselves and are completely dependent on their shepherd. They cannot find food on their own, they cannot protect themselves from danger, and they cannot navigate the path to safety. Without a shepherd, they wander, struggle, and are vulnerable to harm. In the same way, as a follower of Christ, you cannot truly sustain your spiritual life on your own. Without a shepherd you will lack everything you need. That's why Jesus said in John 15:5, "Without Me you can do nothing." Just as a sheep relies entirely on the shepherd for guidance, provision, and protection, you must rely on Jesus for every part of your life. The good news is "the Shepherd and Overseer of your souls" (1 Peter 2:25) knows exactly what you need. Follow Him and He'll lead you to the nourishment you need, He'll guard you from spiritual danger and He'll directs your steps along the path of life. That's the type of God you serve. He guides and provides.

God also provides rest. Ps. 23:2, "He makes me lie down in green pastures; He leads me beside the still waters." This is the principle of the sabbath. One day a week you stop working and rest. To rest is a command. If you don't do it on your own, He'll make you do it. If sheep don't lie down on their own, the shepherd will bend its knees and make them do it. The "green pastures" represent a place of rest, abundance, and renewal. Just as sheep find nourishment and safety in lush fields, your soul finds peace when you trust in God's guidance. The "still waters" symbolize calm, refreshment, and clarity. God will lead you to places of serenity, away from the turmoil and noise of life. He restores your spirit by giving you moments of quiet reflection and deep inner peace. This passage teaches that true rest is not found in your own striving, but in surrendering to God's care. When you allow Him to guide you, He provides exactly what you need - rest for your body, peace for your mind, and renewal for your soul.

Sheep need four things to lie down. First, they need to be free from fear. Sheep are naturally timid. The smallest noise can send them scattering. But when the shepherd is near, they relax. His presence brings calm. Second, they need to be free from friction with the rest of the flock. Tension within the flock unsettles sheep and keeps them restless. Rivalry, butting, and conflict will keep them standing and uneasy. Third, they need to be free from hunger. A hungry sheep will never lie down. It is too restless, too driven by its need. Fourth, they need to be free from pests, from flies and other insects that will disturb them. Flies, insects, and parasites torment sheep and keep them from resting. The shepherd applies oil to their heads to soothe, protect, and shield them. If they're not free, they'll be nervous and won't lie down. If they are free, they will lie down and get the rest they need.

God provides restoration. Ps. 23:3 says, "He restores my soul." To "restore" means to bring something back to its original state or condition, to make whole what has been broken, or to revive what has grown weary. Spiritually, this verse reminds us that God doesn't just comfort us temporarily - He renews us at the deepest level of our being. When life leaves us tired, burdened, or discouraged, our soul can feel drained, fragmented, or distant from God. But He is the Shepherd who gently leads us back to a place of peace, balance, and spiritual vitality. Restoration is not just about relief from pain - it's a return to the fullness of life God intended for us, a healing of our inner spirit, and a renewal of hope, courage, and faith. It's in that restful moment when you experience God's restoration. Today, no matter how heavy your heart feels, remember that God's love is active and restorative. He is ready to bring your soul back to its original glory, refreshing your mind, spirit, and emotions. Rest in Him and allow His quiet strength to renew your inner being.

A question to be asked is how does God restore your soul? Vs. 3 says, "He leads me in the paths of righteousness for His name's sake." He leads you down the right path. It's a path of righteousness, a path of obedience. If you're disobedient, you're on the wrong path and your soul won't be restored. Is. 48:22 says there is no rest for the wicked. There is blessing and rest when you do what God tells you to do, when you believe His promises and obey His commands. Read your Bible daily for it restores your soul. It renews your mind. It brings restoration and wholeness to your life. Matt. 11:28 (MSG) says, "Are you tired? Worn out? Burned out on religion? Come to Me. Get away with Me and you'll recover your life. I'll show you how to take a real rest." Vs. 30 (MSG), "I won't lay anything heavy or ill-fitting on you. Keep company with Me and you'll learn to live life freely and lightly." Restoration of your soul comes when you walk close to the Lord, when He's your best friend and you are His.

One of the greatest blessings in life is God provides freedom from fear. Ps. 23:4, "Yea, though I walk through the valley of the shadow of death, I will fear no evil for You are with me." A heart that conquers does not tremble in the face of fear. It understands a profound truth: the shadows that loom over us, the threats that bark from afar, hold no real power. The shadow of a dog never bit anybody. Why let the noise of fear or the menace of opposition dictate your steps? The true conqueror moves boldly, confident that God's strength overshadows any earthly threat. While the world may growl, threaten, or appear intimidating, the faithful heart remains unshaken, knowing that faith, courage, and divine favor render shadows powerless. Walk forward, then, with courage. Let your faith be larger than your fears, and your steps be guided by the One who has already conquered every battle. Shadows cannot bite; only faith can protect and empower.

We're living in the last days, and troubling times are here. Jesus addresses this in John 16:33 (MSG) when He said, "In this godless world you will continue to experience difficulties. But take heart! I've conquered the world." What's He saying? Take heart! Have courage! Do not fear! Do not be afraid! Why? Because He has conquered the world. Because of that, you can have the heart of a conqueror. Even in the shadow of life's darkest valleys, you are called to rise up with the heart of a conqueror. Trials may surround you, storms may rage, and fear may whisper, but you are not abandoned. With God as your strength, you can face every challenge boldly, knowing that no darkness can overcome the light within you. Fear no evil, for the One who guides your steps is greater than any trial you face. Walk with courage, stand with faith, and let your heart be unshakable. Victory belongs to those who trust in Him.

David next tells us that God provides comfort. He said in vs. 4, "Your rod and Your staff, they comfort me." The rod is a club; an offensive weapon used against lions and bears and wolves. Have comfort knowing God is fighting your battles for you. Jer. 20:11 (NLT) says, "But the Lord stands beside me like a great warrior. Before Him my persecutors will stumble. They cannot defeat me." No matter how fierce the opposition, God is your defender. He does not merely watch from a distance - He stands beside you like a great warrior. In moments when you feel weak, attacked, or overwhelmed by strong persecution, this verse offers reassurance that your enemies may plan, plot, and attempt to bring you down, but ultimately, they will stumble before the Lord. This isn't just about physical threats; it speaks to spiritual battles, emotional struggles, and every challenge that seeks to shake your faith. God's presence is your shield. His power makes you strong and unshakable.

In your deepest trial, God is right there beside you. He has not stepped away. He has not forgotten you. He has not abandoned you to fight alone. The very moment you feel the weakest is often the moment His presence is the closest. Ps. 18:2 says, "The Lord is my rock and my fortress and my deliverer; My God, my strength, in whom I will trust." Vs. 3, "I will call upon the Lord who is worthy to be praised; So shall I be saved from my enemies." The shepherd uses his staff to nudge the wayward sheep back onto the right path. The hook at the end of the staff is used in the recovery of fallen sheep by ensnaring them by the neck or leg. When you've fallen down, the Good Shepherd will pull you back up. This, too, should bring you comfort. So take courage. Even when you can't feel Him, He is there. Even when you don't understand, He is working. Even when the burden seems unbearable, His arms are underneath you, carrying you through.

God is a God who provides refreshment for His followers. Ps. 23:5 says, "You prepare a table before me in the presence of my enemies." This is a banquet, a huge feast. Think about that for a moment. Even in the midst of hardship and trouble, God is at work on your behalf. While storms rage around you and life feels uncertain, He is preparing a banquet that is overflowing with blessings, peace, and joy just for you. This is not a small feast; it is a celebration designed to honor your faith, perseverance, and trust in Him. The table is already set, the finest portions laid out, and the invitation is personal: "Come, My child, I have prepared this for you." Though you may walk through valleys of difficulty, remember that God sees your heart, knows your struggles, and is orchestrating a victory that your eyes have yet to see. Lift your eyes beyond the present trials for your banquet is coming. Every hardship you endured will pale in comparison to the glory God is about to reveal.

David then says, "You anoint my head with oil" (vs. 5). This oil was mixed with fragrant perfumes to refresh and sooth weary travelers. By doing so, you are welcoming them as an honored quest. David is regarding himself as the Lord's special guest. He has been invited to dine now and forever at the Lord's table and to receive His anointing and His blessings. In the ancient tradition, anointing with oil was a mark of blessing, favor, and divine appointment. By speaking these words, David sees himself as invited to the Lord's table - not just for a fleeting moment, but for a lifetime of fellowship with God and to receive His anointing and His blessings. To be anointed is to be set apart, chosen for intimacy with the Almighty. It is a declaration that God's favor is upon you, that His blessings are flowing into your life, and that His presence is ever near. Being in God's presence rejuvenated David, giving him the strength to face all the challenges and pressures of life. His enemies could snarl and roar all they wanted, but in the shelter of God's presence, David would feast and be refreshed.

Finally, God provides abundance. Ps. 23:5 says, "My cup runs over." There are times in life when it feels as though we are carrying more than we can handle. Trials press in, challenges arise, and yet the Lord continues to pour into our hearts. A cup overflows when it cannot hold all that is being poured into it and this is exactly how God works in the lives of His children. He does not merely give us enough to get by. He gives generously, abundantly, and even extravagantly, filling our lives with blessings, strength, and hope even in the midst of difficulty. The overflow is not wasted; it spills out into the lives of others, becoming a testimony of God's faithfulness and a source of encouragement to those around us. Remember, when your cup overflows, it is a sign that God is present, His grace is sufficient, and His provision knows no limits. Receive it, trust it, and let it pour through you to touch the world.

Vs. 6 says, "Surely goodness and mercy shall follow me all the days of my life." God is good always, unchangingly, and abundantly. His goodness is not limited by circumstances or human understanding; it flows from His perfect character. Ps. 119:68 says, "You are good and do good." This verse doesn't just speak of God's nature; it speaks of His actions. God not only is good, but He also actively does good in our lives, often in ways we may not immediately see. In Hebrew the word "mercy" means 'His loving kindness; His abundant kindness; His unfailing kindness.' Ex. 34:6 says, "The Lord, the Lord God, merciful and gracious, long suffering, and abounding in goodness and truth." David continues, "And I shall dwell in the house of the Lord forever" (vs. 6). Forever is a long, long time. God will be good to you forever! All the time! God is good, and He is actively working all things for your good. In the presence of your enemies, you'll have joy and abundance in the midst of a grand celebration.

| 3 |

"LEAVE THE PAST BEHIND"

To be a conqueror, you've got to be strong because strength is the key to victory. There is no victory without strength. This is why you gave to "be strong in the Lord and in the power of His might" (Eph. 3:10). If you have the heart of a conqueror, God will use you to transform the lives of other people. God has placed within you a purpose that reaches far beyond your own life. Through you, He wants to open doors that have been closed, tear down walls that have stood for years, and break barriers that seem impossible to overcome. He calls you to step forward with courage, not just for your own growth, but to lead those around you into new territory. Every act of faith, every word of encouragement, every step you take in obedience becomes a pathway for others to follow. God doesn't just want you to watch His plans unfold - He wants to use you as a catalyst for transformation, to bring freedom where there has been confinement, hope where there has been despair, and victory where there has been defeat.

Your strength is not just for you for it affects the lives of those around you. It radiates to everyone around you so if you're not strong, how can your family have victory? If your pastor is not strong, how can your local church have victory? If the president is not strong, how can the nation have victory? If you're not strong, the people around you will experience less of God than they would otherwise. When you stand firm in faith, courage, and integrity, your family, friends, and community draw hope and confidence from your example. Strength inspires victory, stability, and resilience in those who depend on you. Your strength, rooted in God, becomes a fortress for others. Rise in faith, cultivate strength, and watch as God uses you to lead your family and those you love into triumph. Victory begins with the courage to stand strong. God told Joshua, "Have I not commanded you? Be strong and courageous" (Josh. 1:9). This is a command from God! If you're not strong, get strong!

If the people of Israel have to be strong, then Joshua their leader will first have to be strong. Moses told him to be strong (Deut. 31:7), God told him (Deut. 31:23), the people told him (Josh. 1:18). They all told Joshua to be strong and courageous! Over and over again Joshua is challenged to be strong. Why? Because people don't want to follow someone who is weak and helpless. They want to follow someone who is valiant, somebody who is strong. People are drawn to strength. Not just physical strength, but spiritual courage, moral conviction, and unwavering faith. No one follows a leader who is weak, indecisive, or easily swayed. True followers seek someone who stands firm, who faces challenges with courage, and who moves forward even when the way is hard. God is calling you not to be passive or timid, but valiant, strong in spirit, courageous in heart, and steadfast in purpose. When you rise above fear, doubt, and weakness, you inspire others to rise with you.

Leadership, influence, and impact are born from strength, not helplessness. Remember, the world does not look for the faint-hearted - it looks for the valiant. Be strong. Be courageous. Be someone worth following. And don't rely on natural strength to take new territory, to confront the giants in your Promised Land. Rely instead on God to empower you with supernatural strength so you can live a new normal. Phil. 4:13 (NLT) says, "I can do all things through Christ who gives me strength." Samson's last demonstration of supernatural strength came when he asked God to "please strengthen me"(Judges 16:28). Dan. 11:32 says, "People who know their God will display strength and do great exploits." No matter the challenges you face today, remember that you are never alone. With Christ, every obstacle becomes an opportunity, and every weakness can be transformed into strength. Trust Him, lean on Him, and step forward boldly, because His strength is made perfect in your moments of need.

If you're going to conquer the enemy, the first thing you need to do is be strong. Why? Because there are battles to be fought and won. God is speaking into your spirit today, saying, "I want to do something extraordinary through you, but first you must be strong and courageous." There are gifts inside you that you haven't fully stepped into yet. There are territories He wants to enlarge, opportunities He wants to release, and break-throughs He wants to bring forth - but they require a heart that refuses to retreat. God doesn't ask you to be strong in your own ability; He asks you to be strong in Him. Courage doesn't mean you don't feel fear; it means you trust God more than the fear that tries to stop you. He is calling you to rise above hesitation, above excuses, above the pressure of people and the weight of past disappointments. This is a season to stand firm, to hold your ground, and to believe that what He has placed within you is greater than whatever stands against you.

When you choose courage, heaven moves. When you choose strength, faith activates. And when you step forward, even trembling, God steps in with power. Be strong. Be courageous. Something extraordinary is on its way and God wants to do it through you. Taking new territory and living a new normal is not based on what the will of God's will is. It's based on your response to what His will is. In other words, there are things you must do that are necessary to living a new normal. If you don't cooperate with God, if you don't become strong and courageous, there are many marvelous things that you will never see. Strength and courage unlock doors that fear keeps shut. They lift you above the limitations of your natural sight and place you in the flow of God's supernatural purpose. When you choose courage, you step into rooms you never thought you'd enter. When you choose strength, you walk through challenges that were once impossible.

How do you get strong? You can start by forgetting the past. Your Promised Land is in front of you so leave the past behind. God told Joshua, "Moses My servant is dead. Now therefore arise, go over this Jordan, you and all the people, into the land that I am giving to them" (Josh. 1:2). Moses was yesterday. To take new territory, to experience a new normal, you have to leave the past behind. There comes a moment when God gently places His hand on your shoulder and says, "It's time to release what was, so you can embrace what will be." The past with all its hurts, its disappointments, even its former victories, cannot carry you into the future He has prepared. Let it go, not with sorrow, but with faith. For ahead of you lies a path lit by His promise. Each step forward is an invitation to trust Him more deeply, to dream more boldly, and to walk with delightful anticipation toward the good things He has already spoken over your life.

Let go of what is behind and eagerly press forward with delightful anticipation to what is ahead of you. Do not look back with regret but look forward with expectancy. What God has in front of you is far greater than anything you've left behind. Press forward for your best days, your fresh joy, and your unfolding purpose are waiting just ahead. Praise God for all the miracles He's done but you can't live in the past. You've got to look to what God is going to do in the future. You've got to let go of the bad things and the good things. Let it go and move forward. If you focus on yesterday, you'll miss what God desires to unfold today and prepare for you tomorrow. Yesterday may hold victories or wounds, joy or sorrow, but it is not where God is working now. God is a God of movement. He leads forward, not backward. His mercies are new every morning, not every memory. When your eyes stay fixed on what was, your hands cannot receive what is being offered.

Where you're going is much bigger and better than where you've been. It's a land flowing with milk and honey. You get strong by forgetting the past. Once you do that, you can move forward toward a new normal. The enemy wants to trap you in old regrets, old failures, and old seasons, but God wants to lift your eyes to the horizon of what can be. Your story is not finished. Your best days are not behind you - they are ahead, written by the Author who makes all things new. Let yesterday rest in God's hands. Step into today with expectation and move toward tomorrow with faith. God is ready to do a new thing. Don't miss it by looking the wrong direction. God said, "Now therefore arise, go over this Jordan, you and all this people, into the land that I am giving to them" (vs. 2). Arise and go! When you do that, you'll become strong and your faith becomes active. Each step forward becomes a declaration, "I believe God has more for me than what I see right now."

There is a moment in every believer's journey when God calls you to rise from where you are and step into where He is leading. It may not feel comfortable, and it may not feel easy, but it is in the rising that strength begins to form, and in the going that strength begins to grow. When you arise, you break agreement with stagnation, fear, and limitation. You choose movement over paralysis and obedience over hesitation. Heaven responds to that first step because God meets you in motion. And as you walk, God equips you. He blesses the steps you're willing to take, even when they feel small, uncertain, or incomplete. Faith is not passive - it's a journey that un-folds step by step, and God equips you as you walk, not before you begin. As you move forward, strength you didn't think you had begins to rise and courage you didn't know you carried be-gins to surface. Purpose becomes clearer, and your spirit be-comes steady and unshakable.

Directly in front of the people was a raging river at flood stage and beyond that were seven nations bigger and more powerful than they were. Even so, God said, "Arise and go!" When God is leading you, He'll make it real to you on the inside before you experience it on the outside. This is how God works. This is how God leads. Before anything shifts in the natural God plants a witness deep within your spirit. He gives you a quiet assurance, a holy confidence, a sense of direction that doesn't come from your own understanding. You may not see it yet, but you feel it on the inside of you. You may not walk in it yet, but something in you knows, "This is the way." God leads His children by revelation before manifestation. He aligns your in-ner world so you'll be ready for what He's preparing in your outer world. He settles your heart so you can recognize His hand when it moves. He gives you peace that doesn't match your circumstances so you'll know it's Him and not you.

So when that inward knowing rises up - when the Holy Spirit confirms something in your heart - don't ignore it and don't doubt it. Lean into it. Pray into it. Follow it. Because whatever God makes real to you on the inside is only a matter of time before it becomes real around you on the outside. He finishes in your life what He first begins in your spirit. Joshua didn't know how they were going to cross over but he had confidence in his heart he had heard from God. Prov. 3:5,6 says, "Trust in the Lord with all your heart and lean not on your own understanding. In all your ways acknowledge Him and He will direct your paths." There are places God longs to take you - territories of blessing, growth, influence, and spiritual maturity that you could never reach on your own. His plans for you always exceed your ability, because they are meant to showcase His strength, not yours. He opens doors no one else can open and leads you down paths you never thought you'd walk.

But know this - every divine invitation requires a response. Your part is simple, yet profound: trust Him. When He speaks, believe. When He leads, follow. When He says, "Arise and go," don't hesitate. Take the step, even if you can't see the whole path. God doesn't ask you to understand every detail, but He does ask you to trust His heart. For it's in the rising and in the going that His power carries you, His presence sustains you, and His purpose unfolds before you. Let Him lead you to the places beyond your strength, beyond your imagination, and beyond anything you could ever accomplish alone. God is ready and it's now your turn to arise and go. As you move forward to a new normal, God will motivate and encourage you by giving you new promises. He'll speak to your heart and give you a new promise to stir up your faith. It's your responsibility to listen for those promises and then live in them.

God gave Joshua a promise in Josh. 1:3, "Every place that the sole of your foot will tread upon I have given you, just as I promised to Moses." Get the promises from God and feed on them. Think about them and talk about them over and over again. You're getting stronger and stronger as you continue to exercise your faith. Down in your heart you're expecting the promises of God to become real. That quiet stirring inside you is not your imagination - it's faith speaking. It's the Holy Spirit reminding you that what God has spoken, He will surely bring to pass. Even when nothing around you looks different, something within you knows change is coming. That knowing is God's deposit, His assurance, His whisper saying, "Hold on. I'm working." Expectations born from faith are never empty; they are seeds growing beneath the surface, soon to break through. Suddenly you're living in the promise you've been given.

It is your responsibility to do whatever God asks. Josh. 1:7, "Only be strong and very courageous, that you may observe to do according to all the law which Moses My servant commanded you." James 1:22 (NLT) says, "But don't just listen to God's Word. You must do what it says. Otherwise, you are only fooling yourselves." Be willing to do whatever God asks of you, even before He asks. Willingness is the posture of a surrendered heart. It is the quiet "yes" that lives inside of you long before God reveals the assignment. It is the attitude that says, "Lord, whatever You desire, I am already prepared to follow." Willingness comes first because it reveals trust. It shows that you believe God's plans are good, His wisdom is perfect, and His timing is sure. When your heart is already yielded, His voice finds no resistance, only readiness. Obedience comes after He asks. Obedience is the action that follows your willingness. It is your faith expressed in motion. Obedience becomes your way of honoring the One who leads you.

When you live with a heart that is willing before the command and obedient after the command, you walk in true surrender. You position yourself for God to trust you with greater things, deeper assignments, and higher purpose. Keep your heart open, your spirit ready, and your answer already prepared. Let your willingness come first and your obedience will faithfully follow. God said, "Do not turn from it to the right hand or to the left" (vs. 7). Don't say "yes" today and "no" tomorrow. Josh. 1:8, "This Book of the Law shall not depart from your mouth, but you shall meditate in it day and night, that you may observe to do according to all that is written in it. For then you will make your way prosperous, and then you will have good success." When you align your actions with God's Word, you build a foundation that cannot be shaken. Every decision guided by His truth strengthens your character, sharpens your discernment, and equips you to overcome challenges.

Use your mouth to continually speak God's Word. God told Joshua to not let the Book of the Law depart from his mouth (vs. 8). Like Joshua, you need to meditate on God's Word day and night. The word "meditate" in Hebrew means 'murmur; mumble.' In other words, you're constantly quoting scripture under your breath. You're feeding on the Word and embracing it until it becomes real to you, until it makes you strong. This, in turn, will give you a spiritual mindset where you're committed to follow and obey God's Word every day of your life. If you'll do all that, God says you'll be prosperous and have good success. Not just success, but "good" success. Many people are successful but it's not good for them or their family. Material success can corrupt you, ruin you, sidetrack you, and ultimately crush you. Prov. 10:22 tells what good success is, "The blessing of the Lord makes one rich, and He adds no sorrow with it."

Josh. 1:9, "Have I not commanded you? Be strong and of good courage; do not be afraid, nor be dismayed, for the Lord your God is with you wherever you go." You must forever stay in God's presence because the life of faith is lived out at the deep end of the pool. In life you either sink or swim. It's all based on whether or not you stay in God's presence. God likes to take ordinary people and do extraordinary things in and through them. He doesn't call the perfect or the powerful first; He calls the willing, the humble, and the faithful. All they have to do is continually stay in God's presence. When you feel ordinary, remember: God's power is made perfect in weakness. Your limitations are not barriers; they are the canvas on which He paints His miracles. Surrender to His will, trust His timing, and watch as He does what only He can do through you. You were created to be an instrument of His extraordinary work. Step forward in faith and let God take the ordinary in your life and make it extraordinary.

| 4 |

"GODLY CONVICTIONS"

All men are called to be courageous. This is what makes you a conqueror. It is courage that separates the ordinary from the extraordinary, the timid from the victorious. To be courageous is to step forward when fear whispers "stay back," to stand firm when the world tries to shake you, and to rise above every obstacle by the strength God gives. This is what makes a man a conqueror - not his wealth, not his status, but his willingness to trust, act, and endure. Your calling is to be courageous, to press forward, to claim the victory God has already prepared for you. You've got to have courage if you want to enter your personal Promised Land. You can be courageous if your confidence is not in yourself but in God who called you to go forward and take new territory. He asks you to commit yourself to doing what He tells you to do. It takes strength and courage to do that. God wants to do more in your life than you've ever seen Him do. He wants to take you from glory to glory (2 Cor. 3:18).

God is always at work, shaping, refining, and building His purpose within you. But His work is not one-sided. He desires your involvement, your participation, and your cooperation. The transformation He wants to accomplish in your life and through your life is powerful, but it requires your willingness to step in and engage. There are some things God promises His people that will not happen unless the people position themselves to take hold of it. You cannot sit on the sidelines and expect God's plans to unfold fully. Your prayers, your obedience, your faith, and your actions are the channels through which His power flows. When you yield to Him, partnering with His Spirit, you become a living instrument of His purpose. God's work in you and through you is meant to touch lives, open doors, and create impact beyond what you could imagine but it begins with your decision to participate. Don't let passivity rob you of the miracle God wants to work through your life.

God promised the children of Israel the Promised Land but only those who had the heart of a conqueror were able to possess it. Josh. 1:6 says if Joshua was not strong and courageous, the people were not going to inherit the land. The way you live your life has a profound effect on the lives of people around you. In other words, it matters deeply how you live your life. The way you live your life is never just about you. Every choice, every word, every act of love or kindness ripples outward, touching lives in ways you may never see. When you walk in integrity, humility, and compassion, you illuminate the path for others, inspiring hope, faith, and courage. Your life can be a reflection of God's light - a living testimony that encourages those around you to rise higher, love deeper, and live with purpose. Remember, even small acts of goodness can spark transformations far beyond what you imagine.

God told Joshua to "be strong and courageous" in Josh. 1:6 but in vs. 7 He steps it up a notch and says, "Only be strong and very courageous." He went from being "courageous" to being "very courageous." That's courage with an exclamation point after it. To be very courageous means to be fully engaged, to be alert physically, mentally, and spiritually. It means you're bold and firm. It means nobody is going to push you around. To be very courageous is more than just facing fear - it is to be fully alive and engaged in every dimension of your being. Courage calls for alertness: physically, to stand firm in your actions; mentally, to discern truth from deception; and spiritually, to anchor your soul in God's wisdom and strength. It is boldness tempered with conviction, a firmness that refuses to be shaken by the pressures of the world. True courage is a declaration: you will not be moved, manipulated, or silenced, for your life is grounded in purpose and guided by the Spirit.

No matter how hard people or the enemy try to push you down, you will not be moved. You are strong, you are courageous, and you are rooted in God's power. Every attempt to shake you only reminds you that your foundation is firm. Stand your ground, for the Lord who is with you is greater than any force against you. Keep your head high, your heart steady, and your faith unshakable because you are not just resisting, you are victorious. You're bold enough to say you believe in the invisible, in those things which you can't yet see. You believe it because God said it. This is courage, the courage of faith. The

Hebrew word for "courage" is "amats" and it means 'to be alert physically and mentally; to be brave; to be bold; to be solid; to be firm.' Webster's Dictionary describes "courage" as 'the mental or moral strength to venture, persevere, and withstand danger, fear, or difficulty.' The English word for "courage" comes from the Anglo-French word that means 'more heart.'

A courageous man is a person who has more heart. He's wholehearted in what he does and is not defined merely by bold actions or fearless words. True courage flows from the heart. It is the willingness to give yourself to God fully, to walk in faith, and to stand for what is right even when the path is uncertain. Courage is wholeheartedness in action: loving deeply, serving faithfully, and trusting God without reservation. When your heart is fully engaged, fear loses its grip, and strength rises from a place of faith and integrity. Be courageous, for a full heart carries more than ambition - it carries purpose, love, and divine power. Without reservation give themself to God wholly and completely without knowing where He is going to take you or what He is going to ask you to do. Courage starts when you abandon your life for the plans and purposes of God. It's when God's will becomes your will. It's when you say, "Here I am! Send me" (Is. 6:8).

Courage starts in the heart. To take new territory and live a new normal takes more heart to embrace new priorities and to fight the battles that go along with claiming your Promised Land. Bold faith requires courage. Men with courage, men who have the heart of a conqueror, are first and foremost wholehearted. A conqueror has courage regarding their convictions. Deep convictions in your heart are the compass of your life. When your beliefs are rooted in truth and faith, they guide your steps, anchor your decisions, and give your journey purpose. A man without convictions drifts like a leaf in the wind - twisted, unstable, and aimless. Let your heart be steadfast in what is right and holy, and your life will follow a path of clarity, strength, and eternal significance. A conviction is a firmly held belief or opinion; a strong persuasion that what you believe is true. A strong conviction will make you determined, firm, independent, iron-willed, resolute, uncompromising.

Convictions are attitudes that are treated more like possessions or aspects of oneself. Convictions are not simply opinions we hold; they are the bedrock of our character, the invisible compass guiding every choice we make. Conviction is the quiet, unwavering voice within that tells us what is right, what is true, and what must be pursued, even when it is difficult. It gives us direction when the path is unclear and courage when challenges arise. Convictions define who we are, shaping our values and setting the boundaries that protect our integrity. Like anchors in a storm, convictions give us stability, and like a map in uncharted territory, they chart the course of our lives. When rooted in truth and faith, our convictions illuminate the path ahead, empowering us to live purposefully, make decisions with clarity, and walk boldly in alignment with God's will. A powerful life is lived out of conviction, not out of preference. Conviction brings direction in life. Conviction gives courage.

Living by conviction means standing firm in what you know is just, embracing purpose over ease, and choosing integrity over comfort. It is conviction, not preference, that transforms ordinary lives into lives of power, influence, and lasting impact. The world today needs courageous men like never before because godly convictions and Christian ethics are being discarded like never before. In a world that often drifts from truth and justice, every man is called to a higher standard - a calling to be godly, bold, clear-minded, and firm. Godliness shapes character, grounding a man in righteousness and guiding his every decision. Boldness gives him the courage to speak truth, even when it is unpopular. A clear mind allows him to discern right from wrong, to see beyond deception and confusion. Firmness steadies him, enabling him to stand unwaveringly in the face of pressure and compromise. When a man walks in godliness, acts with courage, thinks with clarity, and stands with resolve, he becomes a light in the darkness.

People no longer have the convictions that prayer is important, that the power of the Holy Spirit changes lives, and that God has a plan and purpose for each one of them. This is why all men need to be a defender of truth, a protector of the weak, and a vessel through which God's justice and mercy move. In short, the world needs men who will not bend to the shifting winds of unrighteousness but stand firm on the unchanging Word of God. For in their stand, God's kingdom advances, and righteousness prevails. You need courage to articulate those godly principles that are important to the body of Christ. Yes, a courageous person has to have convictions. What are your convictions? What's really important to you? At the core of your being, what really matters to you? Your behavior and your time and your attention will flow to your answers to these questions. What do you believe to be true? Live your life based on your deepest convictions. For sure, your convictions will affect how you live.

A conqueror speaks courageous words because their heart is anchored in God. True courage is not loud, boastful, or born from pride. It flows from a heart that has been shaped, softened, and strengthened by the love of the Lord. A conqueror knows that the greatest victories are not won by the strength of the arm, but by the depth of the heart. When a heart is filled with love for God, its words carry power. They lift, inspire, and command the darkness to flee. They declare faith when fear tries to whisper. They speak life where death tries to linger. They echo the promises of God when circumstances say otherwise. A conqueror speaks boldly because they trust fully. Their courage is not rooted in who they are, but in Who walks with them. Their words are not shaped by the size of the battle, but by the greatness of their God. With every declaration of faith, they step deeper into victory. With every courageous word, they remind the enemy that their confidence comes from above.

When love for God fills the heart, courage spills out of the mouth. Such a heart cannot help but speak words of hope, strength, truth, and victory. These are not empty phrases; they are spiritual weapons. They shift atmospheres. They silence fear. They align the believer with heaven's authority. A conqueror speaks courage because their heart belongs to God and when God has your heart, He also has your voice. When people listen to you, do they sense you're a man of faith? Can they tell you have the heart of a conqueror? Speak as if you really believe what you're saying. Let your convictions be heard in the words you speak. Do your words give people hope? Do they give them the courage to rise up and fight another day, to never give up? At the heart of encouragement is courage. When you encourage people, you're giving them courage. When you discourage people, you're taking courage away. Other people are influenced by what you do and say, whether it be good or bad.

What kind of speaker are you? Do your words encourage or discourage? Every conversation you have will either build people up or tear them down. Encouragement is more than a kind word, a gentle pat on the back, or a simple "you can do it." At its core, encouragement is the act of giving someone courage - the strength to rise, to try again, to believe when believing feels hard. It is a holy gift we pass from one heart to another. When you encourage someone, you are doing something deeply spiritual. You are lending them a piece of your strength until they find their own. You are helping them see the goodness of God when their vision has grown dim. You are reminding them that they are not alone, that God has not forgotten them, and that their story is still unfolding. Encouragement is not flattery; it is ministry. It steps into the moments when fear whispers, "You can't," and it speaks with the authority of heaven that says, "With God, you can."

Jesus often encouraged the weary, the fearful, and the broken. His words were life-giving because they carried truth and hope. When you encourage others, you are following in His footsteps. You are breathing courage into souls that feel empty. You are helping people stand where they once stumbled, believe where they once doubted, and hope where they once despaired. So speak courage. Share hope. Lift someone up today because every time you encourage another person, you are placing holy strength in their hands and courage in their heart. You need to be aware that something is happening to the people who are listening to what you're saying. What you say has a lasting effect on how other people think. Prov. 18:21 says, "Life and death is in the power of the tongue." How powerful is that? In a world where so many voices tear down, be known as a person who lifts other people up. Speak words of life to the people you encounter.

Every day you meet someone who is fighting a battle you cannot see. A gentle word, a sincere smile, a simple encouragement may be the very thing that keeps them standing. Your words carry weight - eternal weight. When you speak life, you partner with God's heart. When you encourage someone, you shine His light in their darkness. When you affirm their worth, you echo the Father's voice over them. Choose to be known as someone who builds, not someone who breaks. Let your conversations leave people better than you found them. Let your presence bring peace, hope, and strength. Speak blessing, not bitterness. Speak faith, not fear. Speak love, not judgment. You never know whose spirit you may lift today. You never know how God might use your words to heal, restore, or redirect someone's path. So walk with intention. Let kindness be your language. Let encouragement be your ministry. And in all things, let your life reflect the One who continually lifts you up.

There are moments in life when God is waiting on your voice, your courage, your confession, and your willingness to stand firm in what He has placed in your heart. Faith is not silent; it speaks. It proclaims. It declares what God has said even before it is seen. It takes courage to express with your mouth what you believe in your heart, especially to people who don't believe like you do. It took courage for Joshua to say, "Tomorrow the Lord will do wonders among you" (Josh. 3:5). It took courage for Joshua to say God would drive out their enemies before them (Josh. 3:10). It took courage for Joshua to command the people, "Shout! For the Lord has given you the city!" (Josh. 6:16). Some things only happen when you're bold enough to declare it. This is why you've got to be strong and courageous in your convictions and conversations. When you speak what God has spoken, you give heaven something to work with.

Courage comes by way of commitment. There must be a willingness within you to commit and cooperate with the call of God on your life. God never forces a destiny on anyone. He invites, He draws, He speaks, but you must answer. The call of God is not fulfilled by desire alone - it is fulfilled when desire meets obedience, surrender, and intentional cooperation with His will. God has already placed purpose in you. The anointing is available, the grace is sufficient, and the path is prepared.

But heaven's plans require an earthly partner. You must be willing to say, "Lord, here I am. Use me." God will strengthen your steps, but He won't take them for you. The moment you decide to cooperate with His calling, something shifts in the spirit. Doors open. Strength rises. Clarity comes. His power works with you and through you. When your will aligns with His will, nothing can stop what He has ordained. So make the choice today: commit yourself fully. Let God's call outweigh your fears, excuses, and hesitations.

Yield your heart, your plans, your abilities - everything you have because when you partner with God, you step into the very purpose for which you were created. And in that place of cooperation, His glory shines, His grace flows, and His calling becomes your greatest joy. Commit yourself to being a person of courage. Commit to have a heart for God, to submit your body to Him as a living sacrifice. Commit to obey God's Word. Commit to living in and living out of God's Word. Josh. 1:7 says, "Only be strong and very courageous, being careful to do according to all the law." Commit to meditate on the Word. Speak it out your mouth with every breath you take. Commit to not live in fear. Josh. 1:9, "Be strong and of good courage, do not be afraid, nor be dismayed." Commit to not being discouraged. Josh. 1:9 says, "The Lord your God is with you wherever you go." Be convinced that God has not brought you this far to fail. He wants you to enter the Promised Land.

Trust God and He'll give you strength for the battle. He wouldn't tell you to be strong and courageous if you couldn't be strong and courageous. Commit to believing God's promises. God told Joshua, "Every place that the sole of your foot will tread upon I have given to you" (Josh. 1:3). Vs. 5, "As I was with Moses, so I will be with you. I will not leave you nor forsake you." Faith is not just acknowledging that God can do something - it is committing your heart to trust that He will do what He has spoken. God's promises are not fragile hopes or distant dreams; they are unshakable truths backed by His character. When He speaks, He speaks with all the strength of heaven behind His words. Thomas Watson said in 1662, "Faith lives in a promise, as the fish lives in the water. The promises are both comforting and quickening. The promises of God keep us from sinking when we come to the waters of affliction." To believe God's promises is to anchor your soul in what cannot fail.

| 5 |

"A STEP OF FAITH"

God wants you to have the heart of a conqueror so you can enter new times, take new territory, and experience His blessings in new ways. A conqueror is strong and he is courageous. He is a person who crosses over from where he is now to where God wants to take him. He goes from the wilderness to the Promised Land, to a new season of God's blessings. A conqueror goes from glory to glory to glory. For sure, there are always new blessings waiting for you on the other side of where you now are. Where you stand today is not the end of your story. God has already placed new blessings, fresh favor, and open doors on the other side of where you now are. Every step of faith you take positions you to receive what He has prepared. Nothing in your life is stagnant unless you choose to stay where you are. A conqueror goes after those blessings and takes hold of them and the opportunities they offer. He moves forward believing that what lies ahead is greater than what lies behind.

A conqueror goes after the blessings God has provided, not with fear or hesitation, but with boldness and expectation. He understands that blessings don't always fall into your lap; sometimes you must rise up, press on, and take hold of them. Every challenge you face is simply the pathway to something better. Every closed door is often a redirection to a greater one. And every season of waiting is preparing you for the season of receiving. In Joshua 3, the people are not yet in the Promised Land but Joshua has brought them to the edge of the Jordan River. The Jordan River was at flood stage and was an obstacle that God would have to miraculously take them through. But first, before the miracle, there is something God wants the people to do before they cross over into the Promised Land. Likewise, God wants to do supernatural things in your life but there are certain things that have to happen first. Before God can move, you must first set yourself up for the miracle you are about to receive, before the power of God moves in your life.

Josh. 3:2 says, "So it was, after three days, that the officers went through the camp." God takes the people to the Jordan River and parks them there for three days. At flood stage the Jordan River was a raging river a mile wide (Josh. 3:15). The people are camped right beside it, waiting on God. Every minute of the day they heard the roar of the river, being reminded of the obstacle before them. Every day they had to stare the obstacle in the face. Surely they are asking, "Why doesn't God remove this obstacle from our path? Did He bring us here just to be stopped by this river?" God placed the people by this raging river to show them they couldn't cross over on their own. God even does that to us sometimes. Some of our problems don't instantly disappear and go away until we first are willing to wait on God and follow His lead. We often want quick solutions, instant breakthroughs, and problems resolved the moment we pray.

God, in His wisdom, knows that if He removes the difficulty too soon, we might miss the deeper work He's trying to do in us. Sometimes He slows your pace on purpose. There are seasons when God says, "Wait. Walk with Me through this." Not because He cannot fix it, but because He wants to form you before He frees you. He wants you to learn trust, patience, obedience, and spiritual sensitivity - qualities that only grow when we slow down long enough to listen. Not to frustrate you, not to hold you back, but to grow the qualities inside you that can't be developed in a hurry. Trust is not learned while rushing. Patience doesn't grow while you're demanding answers. Obedience isn't strengthened when you're doing things your own way. And spiritual sensitivity can't flourish when your heart is too loud to hear His whisper. God invites you into a slower rhythm - not inactivity, but intentional stillness. A place where your spirit can breathe. A place where His voice becomes clearer, His leading more recognizable, and His presence more real.

When you slow down, you discover that God has been speaking all along. When you pause, you notice the direction He's been pointing you toward. When you're still, the noise inside you settles enough for faith to rise. This is where trust grows, where patience is formed, where obedience becomes joyful. This is where spiritual sensitivity awakens. If God is slowing you down in this season, it's because He is preparing you, shaping you, and drawing you close. Let the quiet moments become your classroom. Let His presence teach you what rushing forward never could. Waiting on God is not inactivity; it is intentional dependence. It is choosing to move at His pace, trust His timing, and follow His lead, even when your emotions are screaming for a shortcut. And here is the promise: When God sees a heart that is willing to wait and follow, He moves with power. If something hasn't changed yet, don't assume God is absent. He may simply be preparing you for a victory that requires patience before it appears.

For three days the people are waiting on God. They can't cross over on their own because the Jordan River was at flood stage. It is often when you stand before the impossible that your soul finally grows quiet enough to wait on the Lord. As long as the path seems manageable, you'll lean on your own strength. As long as the solution feels within reach, you'll trust your own reasoning. But when the mountain is too high, when the river is too wide, when the burden is too heavy - that is when you'll discover the sacred gift of dependence. The impossible is not sent to crush you, but to redirect you. It turns your eyes upward. It uncovers your limitations so you can encounter His limitless power. It exposes your weakness so His strength can be made perfect within you. It slows your steps so His timing can be honored above your own. If you are facing something beyond your strength, take heart. The impossible is not the end of your story - it is the doorway through which God reveals His glory.

Life often tests our patience. We live in a world that demands speed, immediate results, and constant action. Yet, the greatest victories in God's kingdom come not from rushing, but from learning the art of waiting. To wait on God is not to be idle - it is to prepare, to pray, and to align your heart with His will. Waiting on God is a season of growth. In the quiet, He shapes your character, strengthens your faith, and reveals His plans. It teaches discernment, humility, and trust - qualities that cannot be rushed. But waiting is only half of the journey. Being ready also means being alert and responsive when God moves. The moment He opens a door, shifts circumstances, or gives a word, you must step forward with courage and obedience. Hesitation in that moment can cost you the blessings He has prepared. After three days, the people were told what to do. When they saw the priests carrying the ark of the covenant, they were "to move out from your positions and follow it" (Josh. 3:3).

Life often tests our patience. We live in a world that demands speed, immediate results, and constant action. Yet, the greatest victories in God's kingdom come not from rushing, but from learning the art of waiting. To wait on God is not to be idle - it is to prepare, to pray, and to align your heart with His will. Waiting on God is a season of growth. In the quiet, He shapes your character, strengthens your faith, and reveals His plans. It teaches discernment, humility, and trust - qualities that cannot be rushed. But waiting is only half of the journey. Being ready also means being alert and responsive when God moves. The moment He opens a door, shifts circumstances, or gives a word, you must step forward with courage and obedience. Hesitation in that moment can cost you the blessings He has prepared. After three days, the people were told what to do. When they saw the priests carrying the ark of the covenant, they were "to move out from your positions and follow it" (Josh. 3:3).

The ark of the covenant represented the manifested presence of the Lord. In other words, when the ark moved, the Lord was leading them. Vs. 4, "Then you will know which way to go, since you have never been this way before." The people were told to follow God's lead. Always be ready to wait on God and to move when He moves. God wants to take the people to a new place, but they have to pass through a huge obstacle to get there. As the raging Jordan River roared in front of them, the people faced up to their utter helplessness to accomplish what was set before them. At a moment like this, all the wonderful talk about living in the Promised Land seemed hollow to them. They must have asked, "How can we ever cross over this river?" What these people need now is a miracle from God. They're about to find out real soon that miracles don't happen automatically. Before they happen, you must first set yourself up to receive the miracle.

What has to happen first? What has to happen before you enter the land flowing with milk and honey? Joshua told the people, "Purify yourselves, for tomorrow the Lord will do great wonders among you" (Josh. 3:5 NLT). The NKJV says, "Sanctify yourselves" and the ESV says, "Consecrate yourselves." A conqueror has to be consecrated. He has to live a purified life. God wants people to purify themselves today so they can see and experience His power tomorrow. God is calling you to a life of purity - not as a burden, but as a preparation. Just as silver is refined by fire, your heart is refined through surrender, repentance, and faithfulness. Today, God asks you to let go of distractions, pride, and anything that clouds your vision of Him. Why? Because the pure in heart are the ones who truly see His glory. The breakthrough you long for, the peace you seek, and the miracles He wants to perform in your life require a heart ready to receive them.

Do not delay the work of purification. Pray, seek, and align yourself with His will today, so that tomorrow you may witness His hand move mightily in your life. The seeds of holiness you plant now will blossom into experiences of divine power you cannot yet imagine. God honors preparation. Purity today unlocks power tomorrow. Today matters! Stop focusing on tomorrow. Don't ignore what God is doing today. The Bible says, "Today is the day of salvation" (2 Cor. 6:2). God wants to work in your life today because there are things He wants to do tomorrow. When you purify yourself today, you're setting yourself up for a miracle tomorrow. The people needed spiritual preparation before they crossed over to the Promised Land. Joshua did not tell the people to sharpen their swords; he told them to sanctify their soul. If you'll consecrate yourself, God will do something supernatural in your life. Set your heart on seeking God and living for Him in a whole new way.

Consecration sets you up for a miracle. Before God can move powerfully in your life, He desires vessels that are pure, ready, and willing. Just as a skilled artisan cannot pour treasure into a cracked or dirty container, God's blessings and purposes cannot fully flow through hearts weighed down by sin, bitterness, or compromise. 2 Tim. 2:21 (NLT) says, "If you keep yourself pure, you will be a special utensil for honorable use. Your life will be clean, and you will be ready for the Master to use you for every good work." Becoming a clean vessel is not about perfection - it's about surrender. It's about allowing God to examine the corners of your heart, to wash away what does not belong, and to fill you with His Spirit. It requires honesty, humility, and obedience. When you commit to being a vessel He can use, you position yourself for the miraculous, the life-changing, and the world-impacting work God has prepared for you. Let Him cleanse, shape, and prepare you. Then watch as His glory flows through you in ways far beyond what you could imagine.

To set yourself up for a miracle, you have to purify yourself and get rid of those things that dishonor God. In Hebrew, the word "consecrate" means 'holy; sacred; set apart.' It's a word used to describe the character of God (Rev. 4:8). It's the separation of yourself from things that are unclean, especially anything that would contaminate your relationship with a perfect God. Ps. 51:2 (ESV) says, "Wash me thoroughly from my iniquity, and cleanse me from my sin." Paul says in Rom. 12:2, "And do not be conformed to this world, but be transformed by the renewing of your mind." God's movement in your life is not determined by your timing or your desire alone - it is determined by His holiness. As long as there are things in your heart or life that dishonor Him, He cannot release the fullness of His blessings and guidance. These things - sin, compromise, pride, or unresolved grudges - act as barriers, keeping the divine flow from touching your life.

God is not withholding out of cruelty; He is protecting your life from the consequences of ungodly choices and calling you to align with His will. When you choose to surrender what dishonors Him, confess what is wrong, and pursue righteousness, you open the door for His power, favor, and guidance to operate without restraint. Remember, God's blessing follows obedience, and His presence transforms what you touch. Let go of what dishonors Him, and watch as He moves mightily in ways you never imagined. Crossing over the Jordan River was a spiritual battle and Joshua required the people to have a spiritual preparation. There are no blessings without consecration. First comes the consecration, then comes the blessings. You set yourself up for a miracle by living a holy life. Holiness creates space for God's power to move freely in your life. By living righteously, you are setting yourself up for His favor, protection, and blessings to flow in ways you could never imagine.

The life that honors God becomes the life that attracts His miraculous intervention. Remember, miracles are not just random acts - they are often the natural outcome of a life devoted fully to Him. Heb. 12:14 (NLT) says, "Work at living a holy life, for those who are not holy will not see the Lord." God said in 2 Cor. 6:17, "Come out from among them and be separate says the Lord. Do not touch what is unclean, and I will receive you." The act of consecration involves your life being a living sacrifice to God, totally separated from the defilement of the world. The war you are in is a holy war. God demands purity before He is willing to work wonders on your behalf. You must abstain from everything that will take your mind off of the seriousness of the task before you. Put off the old man and forsake every form of evil. If you'll do that, you'll quickly find that amazing wonders will begin in your life and never end. Each new day will bring bigger and better blessings than the day before.

After the people had purified themselves, Joshua took a step of faith and told the priests to walk into the Jordan River (vs. 6). The obstacle in front of them is not seen as an oppressive trial, but as a glorious opportunity to see God work. Joshua demonstrated the courage that faith requires. When he commanded the priests to step into the Jordan River, he wasn't seeing the obstacle as a hindrance - he saw it as an opportunity for God to show His power. The waters that stood as a barrier became the stage for God's glory. Faith doesn't always wait for the obstacle to disappear; it steps forward into the unknown, trusting that God is greater than what stands before us. The Jordan was swollen, unpredictable, and impossible by human standards but Joshua saw God's promise, not the problem. Your own Jordan River may seem impossible - challenges in your career, relationships, or spiritual walk - but they are invitations to witness God's faithfulness. Step into your river today and God will display His power in your life.

As Joshua takes the step of faith, God encourages him all the way. God said He would make Joshua a leader like Moses in the sight of all Israel (vs. 7). The priests begin the procession with the ark of the covenant some one thousand yards in front of the people. The priests walked right into a river that didn't look like it was going to stop flowing anytime soon. The Jordan miraculously stopped flowing and the people crossed over into the Promised Land on dry ground (vs. 16). One is reminded of the parting of the Red Sea. God brought the people out of Egyptian bondage with a miracle, and He brought them into the Promised Land with a miracle. The key to this amazing miracle was the ark of the covenant which is referred to fourteen times in these few verses. This miracle happened because of the trust the people had in the God they knew was present with them. The Jordan River did not part until the people moved. You need to move first before God moves.

Movement sets you up for a miracle. Too many people are waiting for God to move first. No, you move first. Faith without works is dead (James 2:26). Too often, we wait for God to move while we remain still, hoping for a sign or a miracle to appear. But the truth is, God works through action. Miracles are rarely dropped into a passive hand - they are unlocked when you take the first step. Move forward in faith. Your obedience and effort are the sparks that ignite God's power. The moment you act, God's supernatural hand meets your natural steps. Just remember that movement precedes manifestation. Your first step doesn't have to be perfect - it just has to be taken. As soon as the people moved, the water parted and they crossed over into the Promised Land. They moved before the miracle. They moved before they saw the results they were looking for. Consecrate yourself and get moving! It's your movement that sets you up for a miracle. Stop sitting on the bank of the river! Do something! Put some action to your faith and watch the miracles flow.

| 6 |

"GUARD YOUR HEART"

The people of Israel crossed over the Jordan River when the presence of God went before them. All conquerors must strive to get and remain in the presence of God. Ps. 16:8 says, "I have set the Lord always before me; Because He is at my right hand I shall not be moved." Spend quality time with the Lord. Linger in His presence. Ps. 42:1 says, "As the deer pants for streams of water, so my soul pants for You, O God." This verse paints a vivid picture of longing - a deer, thirsty and desperate, searching for the refreshment of cool, flowing streams. In the same way, your soul is designed to crave God. This verse reminds us that our deepest thirst - our deepest need - cannot be fully satisfied by the world, by possessions, achievements, or the applause of others. True fulfillment comes only from the living water of God's presence. When your soul feels dry, when life's trials leave you weary, remember the deer: it doesn't give up searching. It presses on toward the stream.

Likewise, you are to pursue God relentlessly. Seek His presence in prayer, meditate on His Word, and listen for His voice. Let your soul drink deeply from the wells of His love, peace, and guidance. This longing isn't a weakness; it's a holy recognition that God alone satisfies. Like a deer panting for water, let your heart pant for Him. Let your life be a continual pursuit of the One who refreshes, restores, and sustains. Value the time you spend with God. When you honor Him, He will honor you. Ps. 16:11, "You shall show me the path of life; In Your presence is fullness of joy; At your right hand are pleasures forevermore." There is a joy that the world cannot give and a peace that circumstances cannot steal. It is found only in the presence of God. When you step into His presence - whether through prayer, worship, or simply resting your heart before Him - you step into a place where fear loses its grip, heaviness lifts, and your soul remembers what it was made for.

The joy that God gives is not temporary, shallow, or dependent on good days. It is overflowing, complete, abundant. It fills the empty places, restores the broken places, and strengthens the weary places within you. At His right hand there are pleasures forevermore. This means that God Himself is the source of everything truly good, truly satisfying, and truly lasting. The deepest longings of your heart are met not in people, achievements, or possessions, but in Him. When you draw near to God, He draws near to you, and in that nearness you find everything your spirit craves - hope, purpose, love, and unshakable joy. So today, linger in His presence. Let His joy refresh you. Let His peace steady you. Let His love surround you. For in Him, and only in Him, you will find joy that lasts and pleasures that never fade. Ps. 16:5 (ESV), "The Lord is my chosen portion and my cup." The word "portion" means 'inheritance.' God is your chosen inheritance. Say to Him, "Lord, I choose to make You my portion! You're all I want! You're all I need!"

The problem with a lot of people today is they don't spend enough time in the presence of God. They don't realize that the best place they could ever be is in God's presence. Spending time with God is a choice you make every single day of your life. When you spend quality time with God, the more you draw close to Him, you will reap the many benefits that come with doing so, things like a clearer mind, a more compassionate heart, and a renewed sense of purpose. Also, supernatural direction will come. Ps. 16:7 (ESV), "I bless the Lord who gives me counsel; in the night also my heart instructs me." What does a counselor do? He sits down with you, and then he guides you. God is a Counselor and He wants to counsel you. But first, you must bless His Name. You must bless the Lord with praise and thanksgiving first before divine counsel will come. Most people go to God asking for help without first getting in His presence and blessing His holy Name.

Quality time with God aligns your heart with His will. It shapes your character, sharpens your discernment, and deepens your faith. It opens your eyes to blessings you once overlooked and gives you strength to face challenges with confidence. Every moment spent with Him is an investment that always produces a rich return. Draw near to God and watch how He fills your life with everything you didn't even know you needed. For sure, all conquerors get and stay in the presence of God. The Lord is with you when you are with Him. Draw near to God and He will draw near to you. God drawing near to you brings with it supernatural confidence because His nearness reminds you of who walks with you. You may still see the storm, but now you also see the Savior standing beside you. You may still face the battle, but now you know the Commander of Heaven's armies is at your right hand. Your steps become steady, your voice grows strong, and your spirit stands tall - not because of who you are, but because of who He is.

Ps. 16:8, "I have set the Lord always before me; Because He is at my right hand I shall not be moved." Ps. 18:2 (CEB), "The Lord is my solid rock, my fortress, my rescuer. My God is my rock. I take refuge in Him." In a moment, in the twinkling of an eye, you can have confidence because you know your future is in good hands. There is a holy boldness that awakens in the soul when God draws near. It is not the confidence that comes from talent, reputation, or human strength. It is deeper than that, rooted in the nearness of the One who cannot fail. When God steps into the room of your heart, fear begins to lose its voice. Doubt loses its grip. The things that once intimidated you no longer hold the same power. When God draws near, courage rises. Faith becomes sight. Weakness becomes strength. You begin to move with a quiet assurance, knowing that you are not alone, not abandoned, and not without help. His nearness becomes your confidence, your anchor, and your victory.

Also, in God's presence there is a joy the world cannot manufacture and a security the enemy cannot steal. Ps. 16:9 (ESV), "Therefore my heart is glad, and my whole being rejoices; my flesh also dwells secure." When God draws near, He brings more than comfort - He brings Himself, and with Him comes a supernatural atmosphere that changes everything. In His presence, fear loses its grip and worry dissolves before your very eyes. The heaviness you carried begins to lift, not because circumstances changed, but because you stepped into the One who never changes. His nearness becomes your shield, His love becomes your anchor, and His voice becomes your peace. There is a joy that flows from God that isn't based on emotions, events, or outcomes. It is the joy of knowing you are fully seen, perfectly loved, and completely held. It is the joy of realizing that the God who created the stars also surrounds you with His glory. This joy strengthens you, steadies you, and gives you courage for the road ahead.

Perhaps the greatest benefit of being in God's presence is you will hear His voice. So many people search for direction, peace, and purpose, yet overlook the One who holds all three in His hands. When you draw near to God, you enter a place where confusion fades and clarity will rise. It is there - where your heart kneels and your spirit opens - that His voice becomes unmistakably clear. God's voice doesn't always come as thunder or fire. Many times, it comes as a whisper that settles deep in your soul, confirming what your spirit already sensed. It guides your steps, strengthens your resolve, and fills you with courage to obey. In His presence, burdens become lighter because His words remind you that you are not walking alone. The more time you spend with Him, the more familiar His voice becomes. In the presence of God is the voice that leads, restores, and transforms your entire life. The more time you spend with

Him, the more familiar His voice becomes. And the more you hear Him, the more you come to trust Him.

To hear the voice of God, you will need three things. You will need a quiet heart, a clean heart, and a clear heart. Life can be fast paced. You can be overwhelmed with busyness and activities. Sometimes you feel like you can't slow down. In the midst of a loud, crazy, and noisy world, conquerors must position themselves to hear God's voice and sense His promptings. You must get in the presence of God and cultivate the discipline it takes to get still and be quiet so you can hear His voice. Ps. 37:7 (NLT), "Be still in the presence of the Lord." There is a time and place to be still before the Lord. On purpose take the time to experience God's presence. Find a specific time and place for solitude. To be still you must remove all external and internal distractions. Turn off any distracting noise in the background and banish all thoughts within you that pull your attention away from God. Be still in God's presence because it's to a quiet heart that God speaks.

Ps. 46:10 says, "Be still, and know that I am God." This verse was written in a time of trouble and war. The people were not lying down in green pastures beside the still waters. This is a call for those involved in a war to stop fighting and be still. The Hebrew word for "still" is "rapa" and it means 'to slacken; let down; to cease.' It's the same word Jesus said to the wind and waves in Mark 4:39. Jesus didn't say "be still" on a calm lake. No, He said "be still" in the midst of a raging storm. It is only after the fighting has stopped that the conqueror can be still and acknowledge his trust in God. People think this verse means to be quiet on a peaceful afternoon. While quietness is helpful, this verse is saying to stop all frantic activity, to stop fighting and relax. God is telling you to stop using futile human effort to fight a battle bigger than yourself. All conquerors must stop what they're doing and acknowledge that God alone is the sovereign ruler of the universe.

To hear the voice of God, all conquerors must have a quiet heart. They must also have a clean heart because it's in your heart that you receive divine revelation from God. A clean heart gives you the ability to discern and understand whether the voice you hear is really the Lord or not. Satan comes as an angel of light, and he also will try to put things in your heart. A clean heart is not just a moral ideal - it is the very chamber where divine revelation is received. God speaks to the inner man, to the quiet places of the soul, and if the heart is cluttered with bitterness, pride, or hidden sin, His voice becomes muffled. Revelation doesn't descend into chaos; it rests upon purity. When your heart is clean, your spirit becomes sensitive. You discern God's whispers, His warnings, His directions. You begin to see what others overlook and understand what others cannot grasp. A pure heart is like clear water - capable of reflecting heaven without distortion.

Ps. 51:10 says, "Create in me a clean heart, O God, and renew a right spirit within me." You need a clean heart not for appearance, not for religion, but because the condition of the heart determines the clarity of the revelation. It is in the heart - your sacred inner sanctuary - that God unveils His mysteries, speaks His wisdom, and reveals His will. Keep it clean, and heaven will speak. A clean heart gives you the power of discernment, to know what is from God and what is from the devil. Ps. 27:8 (NLT), "My heart has heard You say, 'Come and talk with Me.' And my heart responds, 'Lord, I am coming.'" God speaks to your heart. You hear the voice of the Lord in your heart. God speaks to people all the time, but many are not listening. They're either not being still, or they don't have a clean heart. The condition of your heart is very, very important. This is why you must now and forevermore guard your heart.

It's what you set your heart on and fill your heart with that determines the course your life will take. Long before your feet ever take a path, your heart has already chosen it. Prov. 23:7 says, "As a man thinks in his heart, so is he." Your heart is the steering wheel of your destiny. Whatever fills it - faith or fear, love or bitterness, hope or doubt - will ultimately guide the choices you make, the relationships you build, and the future you walk into. It's also what determines the quality of the relationship you'll have with God. Having a clean heart also determines whether or not you hear the voice of God. Prov. 4:23 (NLT), "Guard your heart above all else, for it determines the course of your life." Notice it says "above all else." There is nothing more important than guarding your heart. If your heart is filled with God's Word, His presence, and His promises, then your life will naturally begin to move toward peace, purpose, and strength. Set your heart on God, and He will set your feet on the right path.

Guard your heart. Think about what you put in it. Think about what you let it focus on. Think about what you let it love. What's in your heart matters to God. Ps. 7:9 (NLT) says, "For You look deep within the mind and heart, O righteous God." 2 Chron. 16:9, "For the eyes of the Lord run to and fro throughout the whole earth, to show Himself strong on behalf of those whose heart is loyal to Him." A loyal heart is a clean heart. Ps. 86:11 (NLT) says, "Teach me Your way, O Lord, that I may live according to Your truth! Grant me purity of heart, so that I may know You." When you have a clean heart, you open the door for God to move in your life in powerful and miraculous ways. A pure heart creates a clear pathway for His presence, His voice, and His blessings. God delights in dwelling where the heart is clean. When nothing stands between you and God - no bitterness, no hidden sin, no unforgiveness - His Spirit flows freely, shaping you, guiding you, and strengthening you.

To hear the voice of God, you must guard the clarity of your heart. God does not stop speaking for His guidance, His comfort, and His wisdom flow continually. But your heart can become crowded with distractions, wounded by disappointment, or clouded by sin. A heart that is cluttered cannot hear clearly. It's not that God is silent; it's that your spiritual hearing becomes muffled. A clear heart is a surrendered heart. It is a heart free from bitterness, pride, and self-will. It is a heart that has learned to let go of offenses, of fear, of anything that competes with the voice of the Holy Spirit. When the heart is pure, even the slightest whisper from God becomes unmistakable. Jesus said, "Blessed are the pure in heart, for they shall see God."

A pure heart doesn't mean perfection; it means alignment. It means being honest before God, confessing what needs to be confessed, releasing what needs to be released, and inviting Him to cleanse and renew you.

When your heart is clear, peace becomes your companion. Discernment becomes natural. God's voice becomes familiar, like a faithful Shepherd guiding His sheep. If you long to hear God, tend to your heart. Purify it, guard it, and keep it open before Him. For when the heart is clear, God speaks and you will hear Him. You must know and be aware that God does speak to His people. You can't listen for the voice of God unless you're first aware of the fact that He does indeed speak. You won't be listening for God unless you believe He has something to say. Settle it in your heart that God does indeed speak. He speaks all the time in a variety of ways. God speaks through His Word, through dreams and visions, through a still, small voice. He speaks through inner promptings and the desires He gives you. He'll also speak to you through other people and your circumstances. God speaks all the time. The question is, are you listening? To hear God speak, you've got to lean in and incline your ear to Him.

Is. 55:3 says, "Incline your ear, and come to Me. Hear and your soul shall live." Sometimes God speaks in a whisper, and you have to lean in to hear what He has to say. The NLT says, "Come to me with your ears wide open. Listen, and you will find life." In your prayer time, you need to stop talking so much and start listening intently, attentively, and receptively. God is not only waiting to hear your words - He is also waiting for you to hear His. Too often, our prayers become a monologue, a stream of requests and confessions, while the still, small voice of God quietly waits for us to tune in to what He is saying. True communion with God begins when you stop talking so much and start listening intently, attentively, and receptively. Be still. Open your heart. Lean into His presence with expectation, not just to speak, but to hear. Sometimes the answers, the guidance, or the comfort you seek are not in your words - they are in the gentle whispers of His Spirit.

Prayer is not just about presenting your case; it's about cultivating a relationship. And relationships grow strongest when both sides are heard. Today, quiet your voice and listen. God has much to say, and your soul is ready to receive it. Jesus said, "He who has ears to hear, let him hear!" (Matt. 11:15). He is calling for people to listen up and pay close attention to what He is saying. In the busyness of life, it's easy to let quiet moments slip away. Yet, the most profound growth in your spiritual journey happens when you spend quality time alone with Him. Just as deep friendships are built through shared moments, your relationship with God strengthens when you simply sit in His presence, listen, and open your heart. Do you want to hear and recognize God's voice? Then spend quality time alone with Him. The more time you spend with God, the better you will know His voice. Be like the child Samuel who said, "Speak, Lord, for Your servant hears" (1 Sam. 3:9,10). Stop talking and enjoy being in His presence. Be still and listen. When you do that, He will speak.

| 7 |

"HOLY MEMORIES"

G od wants you to have the heart of a conqueror because He wants you to take new territory for His kingdom. To take new territory, there will be things God will do in you to prepare you for what He is going to do through you. Before the victory comes preparation for the victory. For Israel, the Promised Land was not just a land of promise - it was a land of battle. Every step forward brought new challenges, towering obstacles, and enemies that seemed insurmountable. But more than a land of struggle, it was a land of trust. The people knew that victory would not come by strength, strategy, or sheer numbers, but by surrendering everything to God. The people knew they had to trust God with everything they had because the challenges only got bigger in the Promised Land. There were giants in the Promised Land and the people will have to go to war in order to take the land. But before they do, God has a lesson they will first have to learn. Joshua 4 tells us what that lesson is.

After crossing the Jordan River, God told the people to build a stone monument as a remembrance to what He had done (Josh. 4:1-7). Each tribe was to send a man to take a large stone from the dry riverbed where Israel crossed over so the stones could be set up as a memorial. The purpose of this memorial was so the people could teach their children about the great thing God had done, so that the work of God would not be forgotten among the generations. God knew that in the midst of triumphs, people can forget the hand of God that brought them through. He wanted the people to remember, to pause, and to declare to their children the greatness of His works. Each stone became a story, a testimony, a tangible reminder that the victory belonged to God, not man. In life, there are things to forget and things to remember. Forget the pains, the mistakes, and the failures that weigh down the heart. But remember the faithfulness of God, the moments of triumph, and the victories He has granted.

Memorials are not just about the past - they are anchors for the future, guides for the next generation, and reminders that God's works are never to be forgotten. There is tremendous power in having a good memory, especially a memory that holds onto God's goodness. People are shaped by what they remember. Your thoughts, your attitudes, and even the course of your life is influenced by the memories you carry. This is why what you choose to remember matters. When you recall the moments God has intervened in your life, the times He provided, healed, delivered, or blessed you, you are not just reminiscing - you are strengthening your faith. Remembering the miracles, big or small, serves as a reminder that God is faithful, even when life seems uncertain. Your memory becomes a reservoir of hope, a wellspring of gratitude, and a source of courage. Each recollection is a testimony of God's power at work, a declaration that He is still able to do the impossible in your life.

Over and over in scripture there are things God says He wants His people to remember. Throughout the Old Testament God tells the people of Israel to remember their deliverance from Egypt (Ex. 13:3). Eccl. 12:1 says, "Remember now your Creator in the days of your youth, before the difficult days come." Paul told Timothy, "Don't forget all that has been deposited within you" (1 Tim. 6:20). At the Last Supper, Jesus said to His disciples, "Do this in remembrance of Me" (1 Cor. 11:24). Joshua 4 tells what happens after the people crossed over the Jordan River and it's all about remembering what God has done. God wants the people to remember what He did for them, something they couldn't do themselves. Guard your memory carefully. Fill it with the goodness of God. Recall His faithfulness often. Speak of it, write it down, and meditate on it. The more you remember the miracles, the stronger your faith becomes, and the more you will walk in the confidence that what God has done before, He can do again.

Your memory is not just a record of the past - it is a source of spiritual power for your present and your future. People often fail in their trust of God because they forgot the great things He has done in the past. Too often, they stumble in their walk of faith because they lose sight of God's faithfulness. When trials come, their trust falters - not because God has failed -

but because they have forgotten the great things He has done for them before. Remember the mountains He has moved, the battles He has won on your behalf, and the blessings He has poured into your life. Faith grows when you look back as well as forward, when you recall His past faithfulness and allow it to strengthen your confidence in His present promises. Let your memory of His goodness fuel your trust today. Joshua also set up a pile of memorial stones in the middle of the Jordan River (Josh. 4:9). That way, when the river lowered in a season of drought, those stones could be seen and would testify of the time God completely dried up the Jordan. Joshua is saying, "Don't forget what God has done!"

You need to remember what God has done for you in the past especially during times of drought and hardship. Remembering past victories gives you the power to believe what God is going to do in the future. God will remind you of what He has already done in your life so that you can face the future with confidence. Every victory, no matter how small, is a testimony of His power and faithfulness. When you recall the battles you've already won - times when God turned situations around, provided in your moments of need, or gave you strength beyond your own - you are reminded that He is the same yesterday, today, and forever. God came through for you in the past, He'll come through for you in the future. Let the memory of past victories fuel your faith today. God parted the Red Sea so you can have the confidence that He'll part the Jordan River as well. And if He parted the Jordan River, He'll also give you the victory as you take new territory in your own personal Promised Land.

The people crossed the Jordan River and camped at Gilgal on the east side of Jericho (vs. 19). Gilgal will become their base of operations for the conquest of the entire Promised Land. Therefore, it was appropriate that the first work at Gilgal was to set up a memorial to God's great works. What are these stones for? There was obviously a purpose for the memorial stones for the people of Israel themselves. We don't remember the past great works of God so we can live in a dreamland of the past, thinking the best days are behind us. We remember them as a point of faith, so we can trust God for greater and greater works in the future. Faith is not just believing God for what is possible today - it is trusting Him for what seems impossible tomorrow. The same God who has guided you through seasons of growth, provision, and breakthroughs is already preparing the way for greater works in your life.

Do not limit God to what you have seen or experienced. Just as He brought Joseph from the pit to the palace, Moses from exile to leadership, and Peter from fisherman to apostle, He can elevate you to new heights that surpass your imagination. Trust requires patience, obedience, and courage. When you step forward in faith, God multiplies your efforts, opens new doors, and aligns circumstances in your favor. Keep trusting, keep serving, and keep believing. The best is yet to come. These stones would be a benefit to the people's children as well (vs. 21-23). The people were told to tell their children about the miracle God had done. That way they would know that if God helped their parents, He would help them as well. Finally, these stones served a purpose for all the world. Josh. 4:24 says, "He did this so all the nations of the earth might know that the

Lord's hand is powerful, and so you might fear the Lord your God forever."

After God performs a miracle in your life, the first command is not to celebrate, not to boast, not even to share it with the world. The first thing you are commanded to do is simple, yet profound. Do not forget the miracle. Miracles are God's fingerprints on our lives, reminders of His power, His love, and His faithfulness. Forgetting a miracle is more than losing a memory - it is risking the loss of wonder, gratitude, and trust. Every time you remember what God has done, your faith is strengthened, your hope renewed, and your soul reminded that He is still working, still faithful, still sovereign. Remembering keeps the miracle alive. It keeps your heart aligned with His purpose. And it prepares you for the next act of divine power He has in store. So take a moment, reflect, and never allow the memory of God's miraculous work to fade. Let it anchor your faith and guide your steps.

God commanded the people to pick up twelve stones and build a memorial in memory of what had just taken place because He wanted the people and their descendants to remember the miracle He did on their behalf. Josh. 4:7 says, "And these stones shall be for a memorial to the children of Israel forever." Also, vs. 6 says these stones "may be a sign among you when your children ask in time to come, saying, 'What do these stones mean to you?'" Joshua is saying to be prepared because one day their children will ask them the meaning of these stones. Every question children ask carries more than just curiosity - it carries a window into their heart, their struggles, and their search for truth. As a believer, you are called to be ready to give an answer for the hope that lives within you. This does not mean having all the answers, but it means being prepared to respond with wisdom, patience, and love. The questions children ask are important. Be prepared to answer what they ask.

Welcome the questions people ask about our God. When someone asks, "Why do you believe what you do?" or "How can I find peace like you have?", remember that your answer can plant seeds of faith. Take time to listen carefully, understand what lies beneath the question, and respond in a way that reflects God's grace and truth. Questions are not interruptions; they are invitations to shine light in a world that often stumbles in darkness. When someone asks, it is an opportunity to encourage, to guide, and to point hearts toward the hope that can only be found in Christ. Never see questions as a disruption; see them as divine openings to reflect His love, share His truth, and lead others into the life-changing light of His presence. In every inquiry lies the potential for comfort, and transformation. Be an open book about your faith. Welcome the questions. Pray for insight. Speak with clarity. And always answer with a heart ready to share the love and wisdom God has entrusted to you.

Don't be ashamed of what you believe. Don't say your faith is private and personal. Open up and make what you believe public. Faith is not meant to be hidden. It is the light that guides you, the anchor that steadies you, and the truth that empowers you. When you say, "My faith is private," you limit the power God has placed within you to inspire, encourage, and impact others. The world is hungry for hope, for courage, for a living example of God's love. By openly living out what you believe, by speaking boldly about your faith, and by letting others see the hope you carry, you become a beacon in a dark world. Remember the words of Rom. 1:16, "I am not ashamed of the gospel, because it is the power of God that brings salvation to everyone who believes." Let your faith be public, let it shine, and watch how God uses it to touch lives far beyond your imagination. Stand firm. Speak boldly. Live openly. Your faith is meant to be seen.

1 Peter 3:15 says, "Always be ready to give an answer to anyone who asks about the hope you possess." The word "always" means always! There should never be a time when questions are off limits. Create an environment around yourself where people feel they have the freedom to ask you anything and everything that pertains to God. He calls you not only to seek wisdom but to be vessels of wisdom for others. One of the most powerful ways you can reflect His love is by creating an environment where people feel safe to ask questions - no matter how simple, complex, or challenging - about God and His ways. When someone feels they can approach you with their doubts, curiosities, or struggles, you are offering more than answers - you are offering grace, understanding, and the freedom to explore faith without fear of judgment. This kind of openness nurtures spiritual growth, strengthens relationships, and glorifies God by showing His patience and love through your example.

Remember: it's not about having all the answers; it's about being present, listening with humility, and pointing others to God's truth with gentleness. By fostering this kind of safe, encouraging environment, you become a conduit of God's wisdom and a light that guides others closer to Him. Lay a foundation that their questions are important because they are. Joshua is telling the people there are questions that are going to be asked, and those questions are important. When their children ask the meaning of the stones, the answer to their question is that God did a miracle for the children of Israel. These stones serve as a testimony of how God parted the Jordan River so the people could cross over to the other side. The importance of the question is tied to the power of the answer. Memorial stones mean something and what they mean matters. Your powerful answers to important questions must reflect how important that meaning is.

God has a story to tell, a divine narrative that stretches beyond time and space, and He's using your answers to people's questions to tell it. Every answer you give, every word of encouragement you share, every truth you speak in response to someone's question is a brushstroke in His masterpiece. Often, you don't see the full picture, and the impact may seem small, but God sees the beginning, the middle, and the end. When you respond to someone's question with patience, wisdom, and love, you're not just helping them - you're revealing a chapter of His story. Your insights, your guidance, your compassion are all threads woven into the grand tapestry of His plan. God uses your words to teach, to comfort, and to illuminate the path for others. Your answer is very important for it tells the glory of what God has done. So don't underestimate your voice. Even in the simplest answers, God is speaking. He's telling His story through you. And one day, you'll see how every conversation, every shared truth, every answer you gave was part of something far greater than yourself.

Like those stones, let your words be a memorial to all that God has done in times past. Understand that whatever you carry out of a challenge is creating a memorial. One stone is a memorial to God's faithfulness. Another stone is a memorial to God's provision. Add the stone of God's peace to that memorial, along with the stone of God's exceeding joy and the stone of God's unfailing love. You're building a memorial stone upon stone upon stone to a God who does the impossible. What you set up as a memorial is going to be talked about for ages to come. The things you remember during times of trial is what you memorialize. That's why it matters what you bring out of a season of testing and hardship. Don't memorialize your hurt and pain, memorialize the God who brings deliverance and wholeness. Memories build faith for the future. They extend beyond the moment. They remind us that God has been faithful before, and He will be faithful again.

Holy memories fuel holy faith for God's preferred future for your life and the lives of your children. How you answer your children's questions will be told to their children and their children's children. Every moment God is doing things of significance that extend beyond the moment. God is the God who sets people free and He wants a memorial built so people won't forget that. Why did God tell Joshua to have the people set up a memorial? So all the nations of the earth might know that the Lord's hand is powerful. Memories extend beyond the moment. They become markers on the path of your journey with God. When the road ahead looks uncertain, look back at what He has already done. Recall His goodness, His provision, His protection, and His undeniable presence in your life. Each remembrance becomes a stone of testimony, a reminder that you're not walking into the future alone. The stones you carry out of any situation are meant to carry the gospel to the world.

These stones are meant to tell people that God loves them and cares for them. They proclaim that the hand of the Lord is mighty and all powerful. God doesn't give you memories just to feel nostalgic - He gives them to build confidence, courage, and faith. What He did before, He is able to do again. What He promised then, He is still committed to now. So let your memories speak. Let them remind you that God has never failed you and He will not start now. Also, the purpose of this memorial is that you would fear the Lord your God forever. Forever you are to reverence and stand in awe of God. The power of you remembering what God has done creates wonder and amazement and admiration. If you want others to stand in awe of God like you do, then build a memorial to reflect all He has done. Build monuments to the faithfulness of God. These monuments proclaim, "Look what God has done." And the good news is He's not done yet!

| 8 |

"UNFINISHED BUSINESS"

The people of Israel successfully crossed over the Jordan River and the Promised Land is now ready to be conquered. Not too far from where they are now camped is the walled city of Jericho. A great miracle just happened, and their enemies heard about it and were greatly afraid of them (Josh. 5:1). They knew that when God's people are really trusting in Him, then victory is assured. For sure, there is a place in faith where fear loses its grip and uncertainty loses its voice. It is the place where the heart fully rests in the promises of God - where trust rises above what the eyes can see and confidence comes not from our own strength, but from His unshakeable faithfulness. When God's people are truly trusting in Him, victory is not a possibility - it is a certainty. Not because of who we are, but because of who He is. When we trust God completely, we stop begging for breakthroughs and start standing on His promises. We stop panicking at the size of the storm and start praising the size of our God.

Trust is the bridge between God's promise and your victory. It is the posture of a heart that says, "Lord, I won't wait to see the outcome before I believe. I believe because I have faith in You. You said it, I believe it. Case closed!" And whenever God's people walk in that kind of trust, heaven moves. Battles shift. Mountains bow. The impossible becomes possible. Israel has all the momentum and the people are probably asking, "Lord, what do we do now?" Surprisingly, instead of sending the people to war, there was first some unfinished business that had to be taken care of. Before going to battle, God told Joshua to first circumcise all the sons of Israel (Josh. 5:2,3). All the men who came out of Egypt were circumcised but their sons who were born in the wilderness were not (vs. 5). Shocked, the people probably said, "Lord, we're getting ready to go to battle and You want us to do what?" To which God responded, "First things first."

Getting circumcised is a most strange and unusual thing to do when you're getting ready to go into battle. Surely no general would circumcise his men when a war was about to begin. No commander would weaken his soldiers right before stepping onto the battlefield. To do so would be suicidal from a military standpoint. All the men of fighting age would be made completely vulnerable and unable to fight for several days. Gen. 34:24,25 tells how Simeon and Levi killed all the men in a city after tricking them into getting circumcised. Even so, that is exactly what God told Israel to do before they faced their enemies in the Promised Land. Why? Because in God's Kingdom, victory doesn't come from human strength - it comes from covenant obedience. Before God allowed Israel to fight, He required them to renew their covenant. Before they could hold a sword, they needed to surrender their hearts. Before they could conquer nations, they had to let God cut away anything in them that did not belong to Him.

There is a lesson to be learned here. Circumcision before battle teaches us that God is not looking for the strongest soldiers - He is looking for the most surrendered ones. Before Israel ever marched, shouted, or raised a weapon, God required a mark of covenant, trust, and surrender. Circumcision was an act that left them vulnerable, dependent, and unable to rely on their own strength. It was a powerful reminder that victory does not come from swords, muscles, or numbers - it comes from God alone. It is uncomfortable. It is humbling. It leaves us feeling vulnerable. But it prepares us for the kind of victory only God can give. God would rather have a weak, surrendered soldier than a strong, self-sufficient one. The lesson to be learned is that consecration comes before conquest and worship comes before warfare. If you want to walk in victory, you've got to first consecrate yourself and be set apart for God. 2 Cor. 6:17 says, "Come out from among them and be separate, says the Lord."

In the beginning, physical circumcision was the sign of the covenant God made with Abraham (Gen. 17:4-11). God vowed to be God to Abraham and his descendants, and the sign of that promise was physical circumcision. The original command was for all male babies to be circumcised when they were eight days old (Gen. 17:12). It was a sign of being separated unto God, of being separated from all the sins of the Canaanites. These men camped near Jericho were not circumcised in the wilderness like they should have been, so they have to be circumcised now. This was the unfinished business that had to be taken care of before the people went to war. Joshua didn't argue with God about how unreasonable this command was but faithfully obeyed what he was told to do. It didn't make sense, but he did it anyway. He knew that the command to consecrate yourself calls for immediate obedience. Your privileged position as a conqueror calls for the immediate and continual pursuit of holiness.

God told Joshua, "Make flint knives and circumcise the sons of Israel" (Josh. 5:2). God gave this command only after He first showed them His greatness by the miracle of the Jordan River crossing. When you pause and remember all that God has done in your life - the prayers He answered, the doors He opened, the storms He carried us through - something rises within you. Gratitude turns into confidence. Memory turns into faith. And faith turns into radical obedience. It's not always easy to step into places where God is calling you. Sometimes His directions will stretch you, challenge you, or lead you beyond what feels comfortable. But when you look back and recall His faithfulness, you're reminded of a powerful truth: you have never walked alone. The same God who strengthened you when you were weak, provided when you were empty, healed what was broken, and restored what was lost is the same God leading you today. Remembering His power in the past fuels your courage in the present.

Holy memories give birth to faith that will carry you into the bold, courageous, step-by-step obedience that brings His purposes to manifestation in your life. Obedience unlocks the miracles that God has prepared for those who trust Him. Radical obedience isn't blind - it's built on the evidence of God's goodness. It's grounded in the history of His faithfulness. It's the overflow of a heart that knows, "If He did it before, He will do it again." The people obeyed God because they trusted Him and His instructions instead of their own wisdom. They know His ways were not their ways (Is. 55:8). They were in a place and situation where they could trust in nothing but God alone. This command was a test of faith and they obeyed. Because they obeyed, God said, "This day I have rolled away the reproach of Egypt from you" (Josh. 5:9). This reproach was the shame of their degrading slavery in Egypt. The reproach was rolled away by their radical trust and obedience to God, by doing what He commanded them to do.

Under the old covenant, circumcision marked God's people as belonging to Him. It was an outward sign of identity, obedience, and separation unto the Lord. Circumcision of the flesh in the Old Testament was never meant to be only a physical ritual - it was a divine picture of a deeper work God desires to do within every believer. He spoke through Moses and the prophets about the need for a circumcised heart - a heart stripped of stubbornness, pride, and sin, and tender toward His voice. Circumcision of the flesh in the Old Testament is symbolic of the circumcision of the heart (Rom. 2:29) in the New Testament. It was an outward symbol of an inward work in the heart, of a heart cut away from sin, a heart yielded fully to

God, a heart open, tender, and responsive to His Spirit. Just as circumcision set Israel apart from other nations, the circumcision of the heart sets believers apart today. It removes the layers that hinder us from hearing God clearly, loving Him freely, and obeying Him wholeheartedly.

This inward circumcision is not performed by human hands, but by the Spirit of God. It is a transformation that cannot be achieved through our own strength, discipline, or religious effort. It happens in the quiet place of surrender, when we yield our hearts fully to Him and invite His Word to search us deeply. It happens when we allow His Word to cut away everything that does not belong - every wrong motive, hidden sin, selfish desire, or hardened attitude. In that sacred work, He forms in us a heart that beats in rhythm with His, a heart that is tender, responsive, and aligned with His will. As His truth penetrates our inner being, it cuts away everything that does not belong - every hidden sin we've tolerated, every selfish desire we've protected, every wrong motive we've excused, every hardened attitude we've allowed to grow. Nothing escapes His gentle yet penetrating touch.

Circumcision of the heart calls for some things to be cut away. When God circumcises your heart, He is not trying to take something from you; He is trying to take something off you. He removes the layers that keep you bound, the weights that slow your destiny, and the sins that distort your identity. It is a call to purity, obedience, and wholehearted devotion. Before going into battle, God says. "Stop! There are some things in your life that you need to take care of." In the Old Testament, circumcision was a physical sign of God's covenant - an outward mark that set His people apart. But under the New Covenant, God calls us to something far deeper and far more transformative. Today, circumcision is no longer of the flesh; it is of the heart. It represents the cutting away of sin, selfishness, and anything that dishonors or displeases God. True circumcision is when the Holy Spirit begins to separate you from old attitudes, old habits, and old mindsets that no longer align with who God is making you to be.

Let go of anything and everything that hinders you from receiving what God has for you. Let Him do His work in you. Let Him separate you from what weakens you. Let Him remove what cannot follow you into your future. Jer. 4:4 says, "Circumcise yourselves to the Lord and remove the foreskins of your heart." Spiritual circumcision happens when you trust Christ. Col. 2:11 (GWT) says, "In Him you were also circumcised. It was not a circumcision performed by human hands. But it was a removal of the corrupt nature in the circumcision performed by Christ." Just as physical circumcision identified God's people in the past, spiritual circumcision identifies God's people today. It is the spiritual operation of grace - removing what contaminates, healing what was wounded, and marking you as God's own. It is the evidence of a life surrendered, the daily decision to allow God to cut away anger, pride, lust, unforgiveness, compromise, and every hidden thing that tries to live where only God should reign.

Every cut God makes is redemptive. And what He removes, He replaces with something better - greater freedom, deeper intimacy, and a clearer reflection of Christ within you. When the Father reaches into your life with His pruning shears, it is never to harm you, diminish you, or take something away just to leave you empty. His every movement is purposeful, guided by wisdom far beyond what you or I can understand. God cuts only what hinders growth, only what steals strength, only what clouds His image within you. And what He removes, He replaces with something better. Every surrendered desire makes room for a holier passion. Every released burden becomes space for greater freedom. Every severed branch opens the way for deeper intimacy with Him. The pruning may sting, and the process may feel like loss, but heaven sees it as preparation. What He takes away is temporary; what He gives in return carries eternal weight.

This was a big deal to God, and it had to be taken care of before they continued on. God cares about the little details of your life. He doesn't want anything to come between you and Him. All conquerors should go before God and say, "Lord, am I in disobedience somewhere? Is there something You want me to let go of?" Before the victory comes the cutting away of sinful things. Jesus said in Matt. 5:29,30, "And if your right eye causes you to sin, pluck it out and cast it from you. And if your right hand causes you to sin, cut it off and cast it from you." Cut away bad attitudes and the criticism you have toward other people. Cut away lustful thoughts and all sinful behavior. Circumcise your heart. Stop doing those things that displease God. Don't think about it, do it! Cut it off! Delayed obedience means delayed victories. There should be a deep intensity in your desire and willingness to honor the Lord. So much so that you would do anything and everything to see that He is honored.

The old sin nature has to be cut away in order to gain victory in the battles you fight. You've got to crucify the flesh in order to partake of all the blessings found in the Promised Land. To destroy the evil nature of your flesh, it must be mortified. It must be cut away. It must be crucified. Gal. 5:24, "And those who are Christ's have crucified the flesh with its passions and desires." To belong to Christ is more than a confession - it is a transformation. When you surrendered your life to Jesus, something supernatural happened. The old person you used to be was put on the cross with Christ. Your identity changed. Your desires began to change. The direction of your life changed. But crucifixion of the flesh is not a quick fix - it is a slow and decisive surrender. Daily, you must choose to say "no" to what your flesh wants and "yes" to what the Spirit de-sires. This crucifixion is not done in your own strength. The same Christ who calls you to crucify the flesh gives you the power through His Spirit to do it.

To crucify the flesh is not a loss - it is freedom. It is the door-way to true victory, the holy exchange where your weaknesses give way to His strength, your bondage gives way to His lib-erty, and your old patterns are replaced with His divine pur-pose. When God calls you to lay down the desires of the flesh, He is not taking something from you; He is removing every-thing that was designed to destroy you. What feels like sur-render is actually deliverance. The habits, attitudes, and temptations that once held you captive lose their power when you choose the cross over your comfort. Chains that seemed unbreakable begin to fall away the moment you align your will with His. It is the path to becoming more like Jesus, reflecting His character, walking in His love, and bearing the fruit of the Spirit. To crucify the flesh is not losing yourself - it is finding your true self in Christ. It is the beautiful transformation that frees you from who you used to be so you can become who God intended you to be.

Instead of having Israel attack their enemy, God chooses to first work on the heart of the people. This tells us that God cares about what is in your heart. He cares about the inside more than the outside. God wants you to "be" more than He wants you to "do." He cares more about who you are than what you do. God wants you to become who He wants you to be and then you can do what He wants you to do. Rom. 6:11 (NLT) says, "So you also should consider yourselves to be dead to the power of sin and alive to God through Christ Jesus." You are dead to sin so act like it. Get willful and habitual sin out of your life. Stop acting like you're not saved. Live like the person you are in Christ. Remember who you are. The old you - the one bound by guilt, shame, and sinful habits - died the moment you came to Christ so live like it! Sin no longer has ownership of you. Its chains have been broken, its voice has been silenced, and its power has been stripped.

Don't let willful or habitual sin cling to you as if it still has a right to your life. It doesn't. Stop acting like you're still the person you used to be before God saved you. You are a new creation. You are redeemed. You are washed. You are empowered by the Spirit of God to walk in victory. Every time you say "yes" to sin, you live below your identity. But every time you say "no," you honor the One who made you new. You are dead to sin - so bury it. Reject it. Renounce it. Remove it from your life. Not in your own strength, but in the power of the One who lives in you. Rise up and live like the person you truly are in Christ. Your life is meant to reflect His righteousness, His purity, His strength, and His glory. The more you give yourself to God, the less you give yourself to the flesh. Walk like a child of the King. Stand like someone set free. Live like someone who has passed from death to life. You are dead to sin so act like it. And let your life shine with the power of the One who saved you.

| 9 |

"A TIME TO CELEBRATE"

The people are in the Promised Land but now they have to deal with their flesh. The same thing happens today when people get saved. They get born again and then they work out their own salvation with fear and trembling (Phil. 2:12). Salvation is not just a one-time event; it is a journey of the heart and mind, a daily walk with God. Working out your salvation involves examining your heart, aligning your actions with God's Word, and choosing obedience even when it costs you comfort or pride. It is a call to diligence, not despair, to humility, not hopelessness. As you cultivate your faith through prayer, obedience, and love for others, you demonstrate the life-transforming power of Christ within you. Salvation is active, alive, and personal and it must be worked out daily, with both reverence and joy, knowing that God is faithful to complete the good work He began in you (Phil. 1:6). Take seriously the gift of God's grace, living each day as a testament to His mercy and truth.

The circumcision of the heart cannot take place in the wilderness of disobedience. A hatred for sin is what circumcision of the heart is all about. There's got to be a radical removal of the old sin nature. True circumcision of the heart is not about ritual or outward form - it is about a radical, inward transformation. It begins with a hatred for sin, a deep, godly disgust for anything that separates you from God. This is the work of the Spirit, carving away the old sin nature and replacing it with a hunger for righteousness. To love God is to hate what grieves Him. To follow Christ is to surrender every part of yourself that belongs to the old man. True holiness is not cosmetic but is the complete removal of sin's power in the heart. If you are to walk in newness of life, you must be willing to let go of every corner where the old nature hides. Radical change starts here. It starts in the heart. You cut away the flesh so you can depend on God's grace and strength alone.

Heb. 12:1 says, "Let us lay aside every weight and the sin which so easily ensnares us." Not every weight is a sin. Sometimes it can be a distraction, those things that take your mind off of God and spiritual things. Don't let your habits come between you and God. Removing and cutting off some of these things can be uncomfortable but do it anyway. Rom. 2:29 says true circumcision is a change of heart produced by God's Spirit. Deut. 10:16 (NIV) says, "Circumcise your hearts, therefore, and do not be stiff-necked any longer." When you do that, God will move and do things you can't do on your own. After the people obeyed God and all the men got circumcised, God rolled away their shame for once being slaves to sin (Josh. 5:9). The people obeyed and God responded to their obedience. If God isn't working in your life, then consider that maybe there are some things that you have to cut away and let go of.

In Joshua 5:8, we read that as the men of Israel were healed, they became vulnerable before their enemies. Times of healing, growth, and restoration often place us in a position of exposure. When wounds are mended, hearts softened, or strength renewed, it can feel as though we are more fragile and open to attack. Yet, the beauty of this passage lies in God's protection. David wrote in Ps. 23:5, "You prepare a table before me in the presence of my enemies." The men had no strength of their own and this is precisely where God wanted them to be. They cut away their self-reliance and now all their dependance was on God. Even in moments of vulnerability, God surrounds His people with His presence and shields them from harm. Healing is not the absence of challenges - it is the assurance that as you step forward renewed, you do so under the watchful eye of a faithful God. As God restores you, do not fear vulnerability. Stand firm in faith walking boldly into the new chapter He has prepared for you.

Because the men of Israel obeyed God and got circumcised, the people knew it was now a time to celebrate. Josh. 5:10 says, "While the sons of Israel camped at Gilgal, they observed the Passover on the evening of the fourteenth day of the month on the desert plains of Jericho." God is a God of joy, and He delights in celebration. From the feasts of the Old Testament to the joy of harvest festivals, scripture shows us that God is not a God of solemnity alone - He loves parties, laughter, and rejoicing. He delights when His children gather in fellowship, share meals, and celebrate His goodness. And the ultimate celebration is yet to come: the Marriage Supper of the Lamb. This is not a brief moment; it is a feast that will last for seven years - a divine party in which heaven and earth will rejoice together. It reminds us that God's heart is full of joy, and He wants us to enter into that joy now, even in the small ways: through gratitude, fellowship, and worship.

Let your life be a reflection of this heavenly joy. Celebrate the victories, the blessings, and even the lessons God has taught you. Rejoice in His presence, for the God who loves feasts is inviting you to taste a joy that will never end. The Jews had seven feasts they were commanded to experience and celebrate throughout the year. The biggest of these celebrations was the feast of Passover where they remembered what the Lord had done in leading them out of Egypt. Not once did they celebrate Passover as they wandered in the wilderness of disobedience. They then entered the Promised Land and cut off their sin nature. Immediately afterward they celebrated their great deliverance. God rolled away their shame and gave them back the joy of their salvation. David prayed in Ps. 51:10, "Create in me a clean heart, O God, and renew a right spirit within me." He then said in vs. 12, "Restore to me the joy of Your salvation."

In the wilderness, the people didn't circumcise their children like they were supposed to and neither did they celebrate the Passover. Once in the Promised Land, God wanted these two things to happen once again. Speaking of the Passover, Ex.

12:24,25 says, "And you shall observe this event as an ordinance for you and your children forever. When you enter the Land which the Lord will give you, as He has promised, you shall observe this rite." The Passover is more than a ritual - it is a sacred celebration of God's mighty deliverance. It is a time of rejoicing and remembrance, a moment to lift our hearts and declare the goodness of the Lord. Just as the Israelites remembered their freedom from bondage, all conquerors - those who have overcome the challenges of life through faith - pause to honor and celebrate what the Lord has done. Every victory in your live, every breakthrough, is a testament to His power and faithfulness working in your life.

When you remember and rejoice, you are not just looking back - you are strengthening your heart for the battles ahead. True triumph comes from recognizing that every step of victory is a gift from God, and celebrating it draws you closer to Him, filling your life with gratitude, hope, and renewed courage. The original Passover could never be repeated but there was power in its remembrance. The people were to always live remembering that they were a people delivered from bondage. Today, taking communion is how we remember what the Lord has done. At the Last Supper, Jesus gave the bread and wine to His disciples and said, "Do this in remembrance of Me" (1 Cor. 11:24,25). Communion is a sacred act of remembrance. When we take the bread and the cup, we pause to reflect on the immeasurable love and sacrifice of our Lord Jesus Christ. The bread reminds us of His body, broken for us; the cup reminds us of His blood, poured out for the forgiveness of our sins.

For the people of Israel, this celebration was a moment of huge transition. A change is taking place. They're getting ready to step into a new normal, a new future that God has for them. Josh. 5:11 says, "On the day after the Passover, on that very day, they ate some of the produce of the land, unleavened cakes and parched grain." For forty years, they ate manna in the wilderness - a daily reminder of God's faithfulness. In the barren desert, there was nothing to sustain them, yet God provided for every need, day by day. Every morsel of manna was a miracle, a symbol of His unwavering provision. Now, they were eating the fruit of the Promised Land - food from a land flowing with milk and honey. This was no longer miraculous daily provision; it was the fulfillment of God's promises, the reward of patience, faith, and trust. What once came from heaven was now grown from the earth - a testimony that God not only sustains us in the wilderness but also brings us into a place of abundance.

Just as they moved from manna to the fruit of the land, God wants to bring you from daily provision in your desert seasons to the overflowing blessings of your Promised Land. He is faithful in the wilderness, and He is even more faithful in your harvest. Rejoice, for what God has promised is wonderful, tangible, and overflowing with His goodness. Stop dwelling on how God worked in the past. While His faithfulness and miracles then were real, they are not the blueprint for what He is doing in your life today. Yesterday's victories were preparation, not limitation. 2 Cor. 5:17 says, "Therefore, if anyone is in Christ, he is a new creation. The old has passed away; behold, all things become new." God is always creating something fresh; something tailored for this season of your life. Don't let nostalgia or tradition blind you to the new things He wants to reveal. Let go of the old patterns, old expectations, and old fears, and step into the freedom of what God is doing now.

The past is a foundation, not a ceiling. Today, embrace the newness He is offering, and walk forward in faith, expectancy, and boldness. The God who made all things new yesterday is the same God making all things new in you today. Open your heart to His present work, and you will experience break-throughs you've never imagined. Don't resist change or try to hold on to what's familiar. God is at work, shaping your life in ways you cannot yet see. Just as the dawn breaks after the darkest night, He is bringing something new and beautiful into your path. The best is not behind you - it is ahead of you. Trust His timing, lean into His guidance, and step forward with faith. Every ending is a beginning in disguise, and every challenge is a doorway to His greater plan. It is a powerful thing to let go of the past and to look forward to the new things God is doing for you. You don't have to dread the future. You've entered into a new normal, and your future is bright.

Allow God to use change to bless you in a powerful way. God has new provisions for you so don't expect Him to do the same thing the same way all the time. The way He provided for you in the past may not be the same way He'll provide for you in the future. Look for Him to do new things! Josh. 5:12 says, "And there was no longer manna for the people of Israel, but they ate the fruit of the land of Canaan that year." Take your eyes off the manna! Take your eyes off the past! Stop talking about the good ole days and believe the best days are ahead of you. The "good ole days" may have been sweet, but God has not finished His work in you. He is already preparing new blessings, greater opportunities, and deeper joy for your future. Believe that the best days are ahead - days filled with hope, growth, and His divine favor. Speak less about what was and start envisioning what God is bringing. Your tomorrow is too bright to be dimmed by yesterday. Step forward in faith and embrace the life He has planned for you.

God wants to make you a conqueror. He wants to make you strong. He wants to use you in a mighty way. For that to happen, you have to cut away those things that dishonor God and then eagerly look forward to the future. The people of Israel are about to experience the blessings and the battles of the Promised Land. That's a picture of the life of a conqueror. There are blessings to be experienced and battles to be fought. But first, there is one lesson still to be learned. Jericho is looming on the horizon. The walls are high, the ground uncertain, and the battle ahead seems impossible. But before the first trumpet sounds and the first step is taken, there is a greater battle that must be won - the battle of the heart and mind. The people must first learn who is truly in charge. Before you face the giants, the obstacles, the seemingly insurmountable challenges, you must recognize the One who commands the victory. God must be placed at the center, not just in words, but in obedience, trust, and surrender.

Only when His authority is acknowledged and His guidance embraced can you move forward with confidence, knowing the fight is already His. Before Jericho falls, hearts must align with heaven. Before the walls crumble, submission must stand firm. The victory begins not with the march, but with the recognition that God goes before you - and with Him, no wall is too high, no enemy too strong, and no battle too impossible. Joshua was by Jericho and he looked up and saw a Man standing there with a sword drawn in His hand (Josh. 5:13). As a shepherd over God's people, Joshua has a responsibility to see if this Man is a friend or foe. He asked, "Are You for us or for our adversaries?" (vs. 13). The response of this Man was curious, almost elusive. He said, "No, but as Commander of the army of the Lord I have now come" (vs. 14). The Man refuses to answer Joshua's question because it is not the right question. The question really wasn't if the Lord was on Joshua's side. The proper question was if Joshua was on the Lord's side.

"And Joshua fell on his face to the earth and worshipped, and said to Him, 'What does my Lord say to His servant?'" (Josh. 5:14). Here we witness a profound moment of recognition and submission. Joshua encountered the Lord Himself - not an angel, not a messenger, but the Lord of glory. His immediate response was worship. This teaches us a vital principle: all true worship belongs to God alone. Angels, as powerful as they are, would never accept worship, and neither should we direct our reverence to anything or anyone besides the Lord (Revelation 22:9). Worship is not just a posture - it is a declaration of surrender, acknowledgement, and trust in the authority of God. Standing before Joshua was Jehovah Sabaoth, the God who commands the multitudes (1 Sam. 1:3). He is the Lord of hosts (Ps. 84:12), the God of angel armies. This is a military term and it's used 270 times in the Old Testament. It's a name that emphasizes the power and might of our God.

Joshua's question - "What does my Lord say to His servant?" - reminds us that worship leads naturally to obedience. When you honor God with your heart and life, you position yourself to hear His voice, receive His guidance, and walk in His will. Like Joshua, fall before the Lord in awe and reverence, knowing that He alone is worthy of your worship, your devotion, and your obedience. "And the Commander of the Lord's army said to Joshua, 'Take off your sandals from your feet, for the place where you are standing is holy.' And Joshua did so" (Josh. 5:15). The Lord desires all conquerors - those whom He calls to victory - to come low in His presence. True strength is not displayed in pride or elevation, but in humility. Just as Moses was commanded to remove his sandals on holy ground, so too are we reminded that the "heel of our shoes" symbolizes the little height we give ourselves, the subtle pride that keeps us from fully honoring God.

Joshua asked, "What does my Lord say to His servant?" The Lord answered, "Get low. Take your sandals off." God calls you to get low before Him. Lay down your defenses, your self-exaltation, your need to appear tall in the world's eyes. When you humble yourself, removing even the small elevations that separate you from Him, you step into His presence in reverence. Remember: the greatest conquerors bow before their King. The highest victories begin in the lowest posture. God lifts up those who first lower themselves. Get low. Remove the shoes. Enter His presence with the respect and humility He deserves. This scene is so big and powerful and eternal. It's huge and awesome! The Lord Himself is appearing to Joshua and He has come to take charge. He is ready for battle for He has a drawn sword in His hand. The Commander of the Lord's army doesn't take sides, He takes charge! You're either on the Lord's side or you're not. Jesus said in Matt. 12:30, "He that is not with Me is against Me."

Joshua's only appropriate response was to fall on his face and worship his heavenly visitor. He knew the power of God because he stood in the presence of the Almighty. When the Lord came before him, he trembled - not in fear of man, but in reverent awe of the Creator. He understood that battles are not won by human strength alone, but by recognizing the One who goes before us. Today, you are called to the same awareness. Are you facing your struggles with confidence in your own ability, or do you tremble at the presence of the Lord - acknowledging His power, His guidance, and His sovereignty over every circumstance? If not, perhaps it's time to draw near and let His majesty humble your heart. Joshua said, "What does my Lord say to His servant?" He is aligning his will with the Lord's will. Joshua is saying, "Lord, I'm in awe of You. You're in charge. I'm on Your side. Speak to Your servant. Tell me what to do." It's right here that God gives Joshua the instructions on how to defeat Jericho (Josh. 6:3-5).

| 10 |

"BELIEVE THE PROMISE"

Jericho was a heavily fortified city established by the Amorites. It was located near the Jordan River and its purpose was to protect the people from invaders coming in to take over the land. When Moses sent twelve spies into the Promised Land, they all saw the same things: a land flowing with milk and honey, and a people who were strong, with cities that were fortified and very large. Their report in Num. 13:28 was honest, but it was incomplete. They saw the giants before them, but they forgot the God behind them. The difference between victory and defeat is not what you see with your eyes - it's what you believe in your heart. Ten spies focused on the strength of the enemy; Joshua and Caleb focused on the strength of God. Ten spies saw walls too high to climb; Joshua and Caleb saw promises too powerful to ignore. Ten spies saw themselves as grasshoppers; Joshua and Caleb saw themselves as children of the Almighty. God does not call you to evaluate the problem - He calls you to trust the promise.

So many battles are lost long before they ever begin - not because the enemy is stronger, but because our vision is smaller. We look at circumstances, limitations, and what appears impossible. But God sees destiny. God sees promise. God sees what can be, not just what is. Spiritual victory begins with spiritual vision. If all you do is look at things physically, you'll miss what God is doing spiritually. You'll stumble all over yourself and make wrong choices and bad decisions. To prevent this from happening, you must see what God sees. Spiritual vision is not what you dream up in your head or what you think needs to be done. Spiritual vision is seeing what God is doing. It's what determines if you see things as they actually are. When the Lord appeared to Joshua, the Bible says, "He lifted up his eyes and looked" (Josh. 5:13). This verse is saying Joshua lifted up his physical eyes, but he "looked" with spiritual eyes. He had double vision.

God wants you to be alert and aware of what's going on in both the physical world and in the spiritual world. God wants you to have supernatural vision, a spiritual sensitivity to what He is doing. To have the heart of a conqueror, you must see with spiritual eyes. Why? Because you cannot walk in what you cannot see. And you cannot possess what you cannot perceive. When your natural eyes only show you obstacles, your spiritual eyes must rise higher and see opportunity. When others see defeat, faith sees deliverance. When others see a valley, God shows you the mountain on the other side. Ask God to open your eyes and let you see His strength, His hand, His plan. Because once you see what God sees, fear loses its grip, doubt loses its voice, and impossibility loses its power.

Seeing through God's eyes changes everything. It transforms setbacks into setups, trials into testimonies, and battles into breakthroughs. Your victory is not found in your strength but in your sight - in the vision God gives you.

God is always doing something, and spiritual vision determines what you see Him doing. Indeed, God is never still. Even when life feels motionless, even when circumstances seem unchanged, God is working behind the scenes, weaving His purpose into every moment. Jesus said in John 5:17, "My Father is always working, and so am I." That means there is no season, no valley, no delay where God is inactive. He is constantly moving, guiding, shaping, healing, restoring, and preparing. But what you see depends on what you're looking through. Spiritual vision is not natural eyesight; it is faith's eyesight. Two people can stand in the same situation, and one sees confusion, the other sees God's hand. One sees obstacles, the other sees opportunities. One sees loss, the other sees preparation. What you perceive is determined by the condition of your spiritual eyes. When your spiritual vision is clear, you stop focusing on what is missing and start seeing what God is manifesting.

Sad to say, it's possible to see but not really see at all. Jesus asked in Mark 8:18, "Having eyes, do you not see?" He said in Matt. 13:14, "Hearing you will hear and shall not understand, and seeing you will see and not perceive." These words pierce beyond the surface. They expose the difference between physical sight and spiritual vision. The disciples had watched Jesus multiply bread, silence storms, heal the sick, and raise the dead.

They had seen, yet they had not perceived. They looked at the miracles but missed the message. They witnessed His works but struggled to trust His heart. Spiritual blindness is not the absence of God's activity; it is the failure to recognize it. God is moving even when we don't understand. God is providing even when the numbers don't add up. God is leading even when the path is dimly lit. The problem is some people are spiritually near-sighted. They can see the problem in front of them but can't see the victory down the line. Unfortunately, they have no vision for the future.

Joshua was looking at Jericho and was wondering how in the world are they going to take down the city. It was then that the Lord appeared to him in the form of a warrior with a sword in His hand. When He told Joshua to take Jericho, He said, "See, I have given Jericho into your hand, with its king and mighty men of valor" (Josh. 6:2). God wanted Joshua to have spiritual vision. He wanted him to see the victory before it took place. How do you get spiritual vision where you see and perceive what God is doing? Like Joshua, spiritual vision comes from being in God's presence. There is something powerful that happens when you choose to linger in the presence of God. It's not always loud, dramatic, or instantly noticeable. Often it's quiet like dew forming on the grass before the sun rises. But it's in those quiet moments with Him that strength is built, clarity is restored, and battles are won long before they ever appear. Your victories tomorrow are being shaped by the time you spend with God today.

When you're about to conquer new land, be sure you're in the Lord's presence. It's spending time in God's presence that sets up the victories in your life in the days and weeks and months to come. Less time in God's presence means less victories in your life. Every new season, every new assignment, every new step forward requires more than strength, strategy, or determination. It requires the nearness of God. Victories are not birthed on the battlefield, they are birthed in the secret place, in the moments when your heart is bowed before Him and your spirit is aligned with His. It is time spent with God that prepares the way for breakthrough. His presence is what softens the hardened ground, opens the unseen doors, and guides your steps so you walk in the right direction. When you dwell with Him, He equips you long before the battle ever begins. He sharpens your discernment, renews your courage, and clothes you with spiritual authority.

Joshua was probably praying when suddenly - "behold" - the Lord is standing by his side. Joshua fell on his face and worshipped Him. That's how spiritual battles are fought and won. God told Joshua to take his sandals off because he was standing on holy ground. God said the same thing to Moses at the burning bush (Ex. 3:5). Taking off your sandals means the bottom of your feet are more sensitive to what's beneath them so they'll be more careful where you walk. When you're in the Lord's presence, the place where you stand is holy. It wasn't the actual ground where Joshua stood that was holy. The ground was rendered holy and sacred by the presence of God who is the very essence of holiness. Where His presence rests, holiness begins. Where His Spirit dwells, the ordinary becomes sacred. Your home, your prayer closet, your quiet moments with Him - these can become holy ground as He fills them with His presence. Not because of anything you did, but because of who He is. Joshua knows that winning your battles is not as important as worshipping the Lord.

Getting in God's presence helps you understand what He wants you to do. It helps you see what God sees. 2 Cor. 4:18 says, "So we fix our eyes not on what is seen, but on what is unseen. For what is seen is temporary, but what is unseen is eternal." The unseen is where God works. The unseen is where His promises live. The unseen is where your destiny is being shaped. In a world filled with noise, pressure, and constant change, the apostle Paul calls us to lift our eyes above the visible and to set our focus not on what we can see, feel, or measure, but on what God is doing behind the scenes. Everything around us - our troubles, our struggles, our disappointments - is temporary. They may feel heavy, but they are passing shadows compared to the overwhelming glory God is preparing for us. When we only look at what is seen, we become discouraged. But when we look at what is unseen, faith rises, hope strengthens, and peace settles into our hearts.

When your body feels weak, look to the unseen strength God provides. There are moments when the weight of life presses so heavily that even simple steps feel impossible. The body grows tired, the mind grows weary, and the heart feels stretched thin. Yet it's in these very moments when your natural strength fades that God invites you to discover a deeper, greater, unseen strength that comes only from Him. When you feel like you have nothing left, heaven still offers every-thing you need. God's strength doesn't always roar; sometimes it comes as a quiet assurance, a peace that steadies you, a courage that rises from within, or a supernatural endurance that carries you through what you could never handle alone. The same God who upholds the universe promises to up-hold you - not because you are strong, but because He is. Lift your eyes beyond what you can see. Lean into the invisible arms that never tire. Draw from the well that never runs dry.

Don't look for physical solutions to your problems when the answer is spiritual. Standing before Joshua was the preincar-nate Christ, the Commander of the army of the Lord. He's the Captain of your salvation, the Author and Finisher of your faith. He's a trailblazer! He leads the way! He's in charge! He's King Jesus! He's the Lord and Master of your life! At least He should be. Jesus is not your co-pilot. If He is, you're sitting in the wrong seat. He asked in Luke 6:46, "Why do you call Me 'Lord, Lord' and don't do the things which I say?" Look at Joshua's response. "And Joshua fell on his face to the earth and worshipped and said to Him, 'What does my Lord say to His servant?'" (Josh. 5:14). Instantly he is submissive to God's purpose. He is more consumed with what God wants than he is for the solution to his problem. Conquering Jericho has be-come secondary to pursuing God's plan and purpose. Spiritual vision comes when you submit to God's purpose and say, "Not my will, but Your will be done."

Joshua said, "God, are You on our side or the side of our ad-versaries?" and the Lord said, "No." Joshua was so concerned about this current battle that he didn't see the big picture and was missing out on God's purpose. Joshua was interested in a victory over Jericho but the focus of the Man before him was the will of God. God wants you to win your current battle but if you don't understand God's overall purpose for your life you'll lose the war. Don't get so caught up with all your problems that you lose sight of God's will for your life. The issue here is not if God is on your side. The real issue is, "Are you on God's side?" You submit to God's purpose; He don't submit to yours. Jesus did not come to follow you; He came to lead you into the will of God. We're taught to pray, "Thy kingdom come, Thy will be done on earth as it is in heaven" (Matt. 6:10). Your time on this earth is not about what you want, it's about what God wants. His will be done!

Spiritual vision also comes when you believe God's promises. Joshua saw the walls around Jericho, but God wanted him to see something different. God said to Joshua, "See! I have given Jericho into your hand, with its kings and mighty men of valor" (Josh. 6:2). Physically, nothing has changed. Jericho was still a mighty fortress (vs. 1) but spiritually everything has changed (vs. 2). The king of Jericho is still on his throne but in reality, he is finished. People think nothing has changed if they don't see immediate results to their prayers. Not true! If you pray in faith, everything changes. It changes first in the spiritual realm, and then it changes in the natural realm. Just because you don't see anything doesn't mean nothing is happening. One of the greatest misunderstandings in the life of prayer is the belief that visible results are the proof that God is moving. But the Bible teaches us that

God often works behind the scenes; in places your eyes cannot reach and in ways your understanding cannot grasp.

When you pray, heaven moves immediately even if earth doesn't shift right away. A seed doesn't sprout the moment it enters the soil. It goes through a hidden process of breaking open, taking root, stretching downward before it ever reaches upward. In the same way, God often works in the unseen first. He prepares hearts, arranges circumstances, aligns timing, and strengthens your faith long before the answer becomes visible. People say, "Nothing has changed." But God says, "Much has changed. You just haven't seen it yet." Faith refuses to judge God's activity by visible evidence alone. Faith understands that delays are not denials, and silence is not absence. Faith knows that God is working in the details, the timing, the places beyond your sight. The answer may not appear instantly, but trust that when you pray, something shifts. God is already shaping the outcome and weaving together the very thing you asked Him for. You may not see it yet, but heaven has already begun the work.

Once Joshua believed God's words, he then received God's plan on how to defeat Jericho. Faith is not passive for it positions you to see God's path clearly. When you truly believe His promises, you gain insight, guidance, and the courage to act. God's instructions are always perfectly tailored for the battles you face; your role is to trust, obey, and move forward in confidence. For every problem, there is a promise. Life is full of challenges - moments that seem too heavy to bear, situations that leave you questioning, and trials that push you to your limits Yet, God's Word reminds us that no difficulty is without purpose. Every obstacle carries within it a seed of promise, a divine opportunity for growth, breakthrough, and blessing. When you face a problem, don't focus solely on the difficulty - look for the promise. For every delay, there is a divine timing. For every closed door, there is a greater opening. For every sorrow, there is a joy that will come. Problems may test you but promises will sustain you.

God's promises are steadfast; they do not fail. The issue is, will you believe the promise? Trust that behind every challenge, God has already placed His promise - ready to be revealed at the right moment. Keep believing, keep hoping, and keep moving forward, for what seems impossible today is the very space where God's miracle awaits. If Joshua didn't believe the promise that God had given Jericho into his hand, he would have never received the plan. Why? Because if you can't believe the promise, you also won't believe the plan. If you don't believe, you're finished. The bottom line is you've got to believe God's promises. Joshua's faith determined the destiny of two million people. Likewise, your faith determines the destiny of people around you. Your faith plants seeds, and your consistency waters them. The harvest is not just yours - it is shared by all who cross your path. Walk faithfully, and watch as God transforms not just your life, but the lives of everyone your journey touches.

| 11 |

"WAIT ON THE LORD"

Jericho was a tall, double-walled city. Its inner wall was over sixty feet above ground level. It wasn't a big city. It's land mass covered about nine acres. Deut. 1:28 says, "The people are bigger and taller than we; the cities are large and fortified to heaven." Jericho is symbolic of the sins and strongholds in your life. Those towering walls represented every obstacle that stood between God's people and the promise He had given them. In the same way, your Jericho is anything that rises up to block your progress: a sin that keeps returning, a habit that feels unbreakable, a fear that won't let go, a wound that refuses to heal, or a giant that seems too strong to conquer. Whatever that wall is, whatever problem you're facing, God wants to bring it down. But here is the good news: God never asked Israel to scale the walls. He never told them to bring weapons or build ladders. He simply told them to trust, obey, and walk in faith. The battle was not theirs - it was His.

Your life may have walls that look impenetrable. You might be staring at something that has stood for years. You may feel like you've walked around it again and again with no change. But God says, "I want to bring it down." He specializes in collapsing the impossible. He breaks addictions. He shatters strongholds. He heals what was broken and restores what was lost. Just like Jericho, your wall won't fall because of your strength - it will fall because of your surrender. When you put the situation in God's hands, when you refuse to give up, when you keep circling that promise in prayer, you are positioning yourself for a miracle. Whatever your Jericho is, it is no match for the power of God. Keep trusting, keep walking, and keep believing because the same God who brought down the walls of Jericho is still bringing down walls today. 2 Cor. 10:4 says, "The weapons of our warfare are not of the flesh, but divinely powerful for the destruction of fortresses."

The Message Bible says, "They are for demolishing that entire massively corrupt culture." The battles we face in life are not merely physical - they are spiritual, and they require spiritual weapons. God has not left us defenseless. He has equipped us with weapons that are mighty through Him for the pulling down of strongholds (2 Cor. 10:4). These strongholds may appear in many forms: fear, doubt, addiction, discouragement, generational patterns, or the lies the enemy whispers into our minds. But none of them are greater than the power God has placed within you. The Word of God is your sword - sharp, precise, and unstoppable when spoken in faith. Prayer is your lifeline - the very breath of victory that brings heaven's power into earthly battles. Worship shifts atmospheres, breaks chains, and reminds your soul who truly reigns. Faith shields you from the fiery darts of the enemy, and the authority of Jesus Christ gives you the right to stand your ground boldly.

Strongholds don't fall because of human strength. They fall when believers choose to fight their battles God's way - leaning not on their own understanding but on His eternal truth and strength. When you speak God's Word, heaven moves. When you pray, walls start to crack. When you worship, darkness trembles. When you stand in faith, the enemy loses ground. No stronghold is too fortified. No chain is too thick. No lie is too deeply rooted. The weapons God has given you are mighty, effective, and proven. Stand firm. Lift your spiritual weapons. Declare God's truth over your life and then step back and watch every stronghold crumble in the power of Jesus' name. Understand that you fight from victory, not for victory. The Lord said to Joshua, "See! I have given Jericho into your hand, its king, and the mighty men of valor" (Josh. 6:2). At first the Lord doesn't tell Joshua what to do, He tells him what has already been done.

Before the battle for Jericho begins, Joshua knows he has already been given the victory. The Lord said in Josh. 1:3, "Every place that the sole of your foot will tread upon I have given you." He then said in vs. 5, "No man shall be able to stand before you all the days of your life." He's saying, "The Promised Land is yours. All you have to do is go get it." It's Joshua's responsibility to walk in the victory God has given him. God had already declared victory long before Joshua ever stepped foot into the Promised Land. The battles were determined, the giants were numbered, and the walls of Jericho were scheduled to fall. But notice this - God never carried Joshua into victory; He called him into victory. Joshua still had to march, to obey, to trust, and to step forward in faith. Joshua had to swing the sword, and he had to lead the people. The land was given but it would never be possessed without Joshua's footsteps. The promise was guaranteed, but it required participation. God's victory demanded Joshua's obedience.

The victory was not in Joshua's strength - it was in God's promise. But the responsibility to walk in it was Joshua's. And so it is with you. God has already declared your victory. He has already spoken your identity. He has already broken the power of the enemy. He has already opened doors, made a way, and called you more than a conqueror. He will not walk for you, but He will walk with you. Your victory is waiting under your feet. Your job is to step out. Your job is to believe. Your job is to obey even when you don't yet see the walls shaking. What God has spoken is sure, but it becomes your reality when you rise up like Joshua, take courage, and walk boldly into what God has already promised. The victory is God's. The responsibility to walk in it is yours. For us today, Jesus won the victory when He died on the cross and arose from the dead. He said in John 16:33, "In the world you will have tribulation, but take courage; I have overcome the world." Jesus won the victory, and He's given it to you.

2 Cor. 2:14, "Now thanks be to God who always leads us in triumph in Christ." The Message Bible says, "In Christ, God leads us from place to place in one perpetual victory parade." In Christ, your identity has been forever changed. You are not de-

fined by your past, your failures, or the pain that tried to break you. You are not a victim - not of circumstance, not of people, not of the enemy. Through Jesus Christ, you have been given victory, authority, and overcoming power. The moment you received Christ heaven declared a new truth over your life: "You are more than a conqueror." That means no battle can defeat you, no weapon can prosper against you, and no darkness can overshadow the light of God inside you. What you face may be real, but the victory God has given you is even more real. The cross has already settled the outcome. The blood has already secured your breakthrough. The resurrection has already proven that every grave you encounter can become an open door to new life.

Stand firm. Lift your head. Speak God's Word with confidence. You walk in a grace that empowers, a strength that sustains, and a victory that never fades. The enemy wants you to see yourself as weak, defeated, or overwhelmed but God says, "You are My child, My warrior, and My victor." Walk in that truth today. Let faith rise. Let boldness grow. Let the world see what heaven already knows: You are not a victim. You are a victor in Christ Jesus. And the victory is already yours. Eph. 1:3 says Christ "has blessed us with every spiritual blessing in the heavenly places in Christ." 2 Peter 1:3 says, "His divine power has given to us all things that pertain to life and godliness." The victory is yours and you have everything to tear down the walls of Jericho in your life. Rom. 8:37, "But in all these things we overwhelmingly conquer through Him who loved us." In Christ, you're dead to sin and alive to God (Rom. 6:11). You are a super conqueror in Jesus Christ.

To overtake Jericho, the people had to silently march around the city one time each day over a period of six days (Josh. 6:3). Then, on the seventh day, they were to march around the city seven times, after which the priests would blow their trumpets (vs. 4). Vs. 5 says, "Then it shall come to pass, when they make a long blast of the ram's horn, and when you hear the sound of the trumpet, that all shall shout with a great shout." There comes a moment in every believer's life when God signals that the season of silence is over. For a time, He may have you walking quietly, circling walls you cannot move, facing obstacles you cannot shake, and enduring seasons you cannot understand. Yet heaven knows the appointed time. God always has a set moment when He says, "Now shout." The long blast of the ram's horn was not just noise - it was a divine announcement. It meant God was stepping in. It meant the struggle was ending. It meant the wall had no right to stand any longer.

The trumpet's sound carried a message to every heart: Prepare for breakthrough. Prepare for victory. Prepare for what God is about to do. And when the people lifted their voices with a great shout, they weren't shouting in their own strength. They were shouting in agreement with God's promise. Their shout was a shout of faith, a shout of obedience, a shout that said, "God, we believe You. We trust You. We align with what You have declared." What happens next? "Then the wall of the city will fall down flat. And the people shall go up every man straight before him" (vs. 5). Your shout today may not be loud with your lips, but it can be loud in your spirit. It is the shout of prayer, the shout of praise, the shout of unwavering confidence that God is faithful. So when God stirs your heart, when He confirms His word, when He breathes courage back into your soul - lift up your faith and shout. For on the other side of that shout are walls falling, chains breaking, and victories you could never win on your own.

The Jews had two types of trumpets: the silver trumpet and the ram's horn. The silver trumpet was used to sound an alarm. It was used as a call to war. The ram's horn is known as a "shofar" and was used primarily to signal a time of celebration. The priests didn't blow a silver trumpet to declare war against Jericho. The priests weren't calling the forces into battle; they were declaring that the victory had already been won. Blowing the ram's horn was not a call to war, it was a call to celebrate. It announced the arrival of God's presence, the declaration of freedom, the beginning of a new season, the celebration of victory already won. When the horn sounded, it was a reminder that God had gone before His people. It was not a signal to brace themselves, but to lift their heads. Not a cry of fear, but a shout of faith. The ram's horn declares that God has already made a way, that the battle is the Lord's. It was a time to rejoice for God is welcoming the people into a season of victory, restoration, and breakthrough.

Understand that you overcome your Jericho through faith and patience. Heb. 6:12 says to "imitate those who through faith and patience inherit the promises." God gave Joshua the battle plan. For six days they were to march around the city one time. On the seventh day, they were to march around the city seven times, after which the priests would blow the ram's horn. The people would then shout a great shout, and the walls would fall down at that time. For sure, this was a strange battle plan. Nonetheless, Joshua didn't question God but faithfully obeyed. You don't need faith to do things that are reasonable, you need faith to do what is unreasonable. Prov. 3:5 says, "Trust in the Lord with all your heart and lean not on your own understanding." Do what God tells you to do even when it seems crazy and makes no sense to you. Joshua did exactly what God told him to do and gained the victory through faith and patience.

God said in Is. 55:8, "For My thoughts are not your thoughts, neither are your ways My ways." God is saying, "I don't think like you do. My plans are different than yours." By faith you need to obey what doesn't seem normal or rational to you. There will be moments in your walk with God when obedience won't make sense. His instructions may stretch your thinking, defy your logic, and challenge what feels comfortable or familiar. But faith was never meant to fit inside the boundaries of human reasoning. Faith steps beyond what is normal and reaches for what is supernatural. Noah had never seen rain, yet he built an ark. Abraham had no map, yet he left everything to follow God's voice. Peter had no guarantee, yet he stepped out of the boat. God's greatest works are often hidden on the other side of instructions that don't seem rational to us. When you choose to obey anyway simply because He said so, you position yourself for divine intervention, divine direction, and divine breakthroughs.

Obedience that makes no sense to the mind often makes perfect sense to heaven. So when God nudges your spirit, even if the command feels unusual or uncomfortable, trust Him. Move forward. Do the thing that doesn't seem normal. Because your miracle is usually wrapped in an instruction that requires faith, not understanding. Walk boldly and obey fearlessly. God will honor the faith that dares to obey the impossible. There are moments in your walk with God when He will ask you to step into places that make no sense to the natural mind. He will call you to trust beyond logic, to obey beyond comfort, and to believe beyond what your eyes can see. These are the moments when faith becomes more than a confession - these are the moments when faith becomes obedience. God is asking, "Are you going to do what I say or not?" It takes a step of faith to obtain the promises of God. When you do what God tells you to do, He'll part rivers and tear down walls. When you do your part, He'll do His part.

Why did God tell the people to march around Jericho for seven days? Because "seven" is the number of completeness and God wanted them to wait for the victory. By faith and patience you inherit the promises of God. Most problems don't go away as fast and as soon as you'd like. It takes faith to do things God's way. It takes patience to wait on God's timing. The people marched around Jericho the first day, but the walls were still standing. Neither did the walls fall on the second through the sixth day. Those in faith keep walking even when the walls have not yet fallen. Don't be impatient like Abraham who created an Ishmael but keep walking. Don't give up! Don't quit! Press on! Keep walking! Every step in faith is a step into God's purpose. Remember that God never called you to run in your own strength - He called you to walk with Him, step by step, moment by moment. Ps. 127:14 says, "Wait on the Lord; Be of good courage, and he shall strengthen your heart; Wait, I say, on the Lord!"

Walk forward with courage, knowing the One who walks with you never stumbles, never sleeps, and never lets go. Your story isn't over. Your miracle is still in motion. Press on for God is not finished with you yet. As you march around your Jericho understand that God is faithful and expects obedience. Rest assured, God is faithful to keep His word (Heb. 10:23). He is the ultimate promise keeper. He always does what He says He is going to do in His timing. In Rev. 19:11, Jesus is called "Faithful and True." This title reveals His character and expresses the total trustworthiness and constancy of our Lord. It emphasizes the complete reliability of God. He can be trusted to complete the good work He began (Phil.1:6). The people were told to march around Jericho in silence for seven days (Josh. 6:10).They couldn't say anything, and God expected them to obey this command. On the seventh day, after marching around the city seven times, they shouted a great shout, and the walls fell down.

Josh. 6:27 says, "So the Lord was with Joshua, and his fame spread throughout all the country!" What made Joshua such a great man? Obedience! He obeyed the Lord! He did what God told him to do and you must do the same thing. Obedience is an essential part of the Christian faith. The Bible says we show our love for God by obeying Him in all things. For sure, love is proven through obedience. The Bible makes it clear that your love for God is not measured merely by your words, emotions, or intentions - it is revealed through your obedience. Jesus said, "If you love Me, keep My commandments" (John 14:15). Obedience is the language of love spoken from the heart of a true believer. When you obey God, you are declaring, "Lord, I trust You more than I trust myself. Your way is better than my way. Your wisdom is higher than my understanding. Every act of obedience - whether big or small - is an offering of love laid at His feet.

Obedience is not bondage; it is freedom. It aligns your life with God's perfect will and opens the door for blessing, protection, and intimacy with Him. The more you walk in His Word, the more clearly you will see His hand guiding, strengthening, and shaping your life. To obey God is to love Him with action. It is to let your life reflect His truth, honor His authority, and reveal His character to the world. So today, walk in obedience - not out of fear or obligation, but out of love. Because the greatest expression of love toward God is a surrendered, willing, and obedient heart. It is your obligation to obey Him just as Jesus was "obedient unto death, even the death on a cross" (Phil. 2:8). Obedience is the response God seeks from you because it shows He is first in your life above all others. You can be a great person of faith if you'll just say "Yes, Lord" and do what He says. If you'll do that, God will bless you and you'll walk in victory.

| 12 |

"THE SHOUT OF PRAISE"

God gave Jericho into the hands of the people but there were things they had to do if they were going to see the victory. God will require some things of you that will require a step of faith. 2 Cor. 5:7 says we walk by faith, not by sight. Sight keeps us grounded in what is. Faith reaches for what can be through the power of God. Sight shows you limitations. Faith reveals possibilities. Sight looks at the storm. Faith sees the Savior standing above the waves. Faith sees the invisible and believes for the impossible. Every promise of God contains a step of faith. Abraham had to leave his home. Peter had to step out of the boat. Joshua had to march around the walls. None of them had guarantees - only God's voice and God's Word. And that was enough. What happens next may not be revealed until you take your next step. Faith is not about having all the answers. It's about trusting the One who does. Sometimes God won't show you the entire road because He wants to walk it with you, one step at a time.

If God is requiring something from you that stretches you - don't shrink back. Move forward. Lean into His strength. Step out, even if your knees are trembling. Because when you take a step of faith, heaven moves with you. Josh. 6:3 says, "You shall march around the city, all you men of war; you shall go around the city once. This you shall do six days." The men marched by faith even though each day the walls were still standing. The people were told to march in silence so they wouldn't speak doubt because the walls had not yet fallen. There are moments in life when your heart feels heavy, your mind is overwhelmed, and your tongue is tempted to speak from fear, frustration, or doubt. But the Word of God teaches us a powerful principle: if you cannot speak in faith, it is better to be silent. Silence is not weakness - it is wisdom. Words carry power (Prov. 18:21). They shape the atmosphere around you, influence the direction of your thoughts, and even impacts the strength of your faith.

There will be times when you don't feel like declaring God's promises. In those moments, instead of letting negativity escape your mouth, choose silence. Even Jesus stayed silent before His accusers (Isaiah 53:7) showing us that silence can be a shield when the right words aren't ready. He who was the Word chose no words in that moment. Not because He lacked power. Not because He had no defense. But because silence was His strength, His shield, and His obedience to the Father's plan. Sometimes the most spiritual thing you can do is hold your peace and say nothing. If the Son of God could trust the Father enough to stay silent, so can you. If you find yourself in a season where faith-filled words aren't at the tip of your tongue yet, then pause. Stand still and trust God. Let Him minister to your heart. Let your silence be a shield. Let your restraint be worship. And when the right words come in God's timing, they will carry power, purpose, and peace.

On the seventh day the men would circle the city seven times. The priests then blew the trumpets, and the men shouted a great shout. How did God bring about this victory? With a sword? No! With a spear? No! With a battering ram? No! The weapon He chose was a shout. The shout of a conqueror is a shout of praise. One of the keys to living an overflowing life where you see impossible things happen is praise. In other words, praise paves the way. In this chapter, the word "shout" or "shouted" is repeated nine times. This is a passage about shouting the shout of praise. The Hebrew word for "shout" is "ruwa" and it means 'to split the ears with sound.' This is a word of praise, of celebration, a word of lifting your voice to the Lord. A shout of praise is a spiritual weapon that brings about the victory. This is why all conquerors need to lift their voice to the Lord and shout a shout of praise. A dead church is a silent church because where there is no celebration of praise, there is a diminishing of spiritual victory and power.

The shout of praise is found throughout all of scripture, and it should be found in your life as well. You can't keep quiet when God has set your heart on fire. True excitement for Him bursts from within. It spills into your words, your actions, your joy. When God moves in your life, silence is not an option; your praise, your testimony, your faith becomes a beacon for others. Let your excitement for God be louder than fear, stronger than hesitation, and brighter than doubt. Speak, sing, live, and shine because a heart on fire for God cannot stay silent. Praise is more than words; it is an exuberant celebration of God's goodness. It bursts forth with lively energy, filling the heart and atmosphere with joy, excitement, and gratitude. When we praise, we lift our voices, our hands, and our spirits in unrestrained adoration, declaring God's greatness over our lives. It is a spiritual expression that transforms heaviness into joy, sorrow into triumph, and the ordinary into a divine encounter.

Let your praise be bold and full of life, for God inhabits the praises of His people. Celebrate Him with enthusiasm, dance in His presence, and let the vibrancy of your heart reflect the glory of His love. True praise is infectious - it inspires others, strengthens faith, and invites the Holy Spirit to move powerfully. Rejoice! Let your praise be a living, breathing testimony of God's faithfulness and the delight of a heart set free in His presence. Indeed, the outcome of your battle is tied to your shout of praise. Ps. 108:9 (ESV) says, "I shout in triumph." It's when you shout with praise that God shows Himself powerful in a special way. The bottom line is, get excited about God. Shout out loud, "Hallelujah! Praise the Lord! Glory to Your holy Name!" Ps. 81:1 says, "Sing for joy to God our strength; shout aloud to the God of Jacob!" Notice it says to shout "aloud." People say they're silent on the outside but shouting on the inside. Wrong! You can't shout aloud in silence! A joyful shout is heard on the outside.

Yes, the shout of praise is loud. Josh. 6:5 calls it a "great shout." Why do you shout aloud? "For the Lord is great, and greatly to be praised" (Ps. 96:4). Make no mistake about it, the volume of your praise matters to God. You don't praise Him with a whisper. Too often, we think God is pleased with quiet, polite murmurs of thanks. But Scripture and experience tell us otherwise. When you praise God, He wants the fullness of your heart expressed boldly, loudly, and unreservedly. Your voice - your enthusiasm, your joy, your surrender - matters. A whisper cannot shake the heavens, but a resounding praise can. When David danced before the Lord with all his might, when the Israelites shouted at Jericho, when Paul and Silas sang in the prison - God moved. He honors praise that is fearless and unrestrained. Don't be afraid to lift your voice. Don't let timidity silence your worship. Instead, praise Him with boldness. Praise Him with passion. Praise Him with everything you are.

God hears when you praise Him and He is moved by the sound of a life unafraid to worship Him. Get out of your comfort zone and stop praising God in a whisper. Shout aloud! The spiritual edge of the sword and the tip of the spear was the worshipping shout of the people. Ps. 47:1 says, "Oh, clap your hands, all you peoples! Shout to God with the voice of triumph!" The ESV says, "Shout to God with loud songs of joy!" There is something powerful about lifting up a loud shout of praise. When your voice rises, unrestrained and wholehearted, it breaks through the heaviness of doubt, fear, and discouragement. A shout of praise is a declaration that God is greater than your circumstances, stronger than your struggles, and worthy of your adoration. In that moment, the atmosphere shifts. Heaven leans in. Chains are broken. Joy is released. Lift your voice boldly, lift your hands freely, and let your spirit declare the goodness of God because there is supernatural power in a shout of praise.

Conquerors understand the power of their shout. The heart of a conqueror says, "My shouts of praise are going to get louder than the battle I'm facing." They know that praise is a spiritual weapon that tears down strongholds. Praise is more than a song and far more than a warm feeling. Praise is a weapon - a mighty, God-given instrument that demolishes strongholds, confuses the enemy, and shifts the atmosphere in favor of God's people. Praise does not wait for circumstances to improve - it changes the battlefield itself. It turns despair into hope, fear into faith, and heaviness into joy. In the midst of trials, when the walls seem unbreakable and the enemy seems relentless, praise is our mighty hammer, striking on behalf of God's people and opening the doors for breakthrough. The more the enemy tries to intimidate you, the louder your praise should rise because praise is not powerless; it is a weapon of the Almighty. In the praises of His people, His power is made manifest.

Your own personal Jericho can come in all shapes and sizes. It can be physical, emotional, financial, or relational. How do you bring down these strongholds? You walk in faith and use the shout of praise as a spiritual weapon. Strongholds in your life - those deep-rooted fears, doubts, and challenges - cannot withstand the power of unwavering faith. To bring them down, you must first walk in faith, trusting not in your own strength, but in the One who fights for you. Faith positions you in victory even when the battle seems impossible. But faith alone is not passive; it is active, and one of the most powerful expressions of faith is praise. The Bible shows us that victory belongs to those who praise and worship with a fearless heart. Know with certainty that the strongholds in your life will crumble when you lift your voice in worship, declaring God's power, goodness, and faithfulness. Let your praise shake the foundations of every obstacle, every fear, and every enemy that seeks to hold you captive.

Ps. 149:6 says, "May the praise of God be in their mouth and a double-edged sword in their hands." Our battles are spiritual, and you need spiritual weapons to win the victory. You can't win a spiritual battle with physical weapons. 2 Cor. 10:3 says, "For though we live in the world, we do not wage war as the world does." Vs. 4 (NIV), "The weapons we fight with are not the weapons of the world. On the contrary, they have divine power to demolish strongholds." Praise is a weapon so exercise it boldly. Praise pushes back darkness. It shakes the strongholds of worry. It opens the heavens and invites God's presence into your situation. The moment you begin to praise, even in the midst of trials, you shift your focus from the problem to the Provider. So, don't hold back. Praise Him loudly. Praise Him boldly. Praise Him in every circumstance, for your praise releases heaven's power on your behalf. Use it mightily, and watch mountains move, chains break, and victory unfold.

Joshua obeyed the Lord and instructed Israel to destroy Jericho using divinely powerful weapons. Josh. 6:20 says, "The people shouted with a great shout and the wall fell down flat." When life places obstacles in your path, it can feel as though every door is shut and every way forward is blocked. But there is a weapon far greater than any problem, stronger than any wall, and more powerful than any enemy. No barrier can withstand the power of praise. It's praise that defeats the enemy. Praise is not just words; it is a declaration of faith, a spiritual force that shifts atmospheres and breaks chains. The enemy trembles when praise rises because it calls on the presence of God, turning impossibilities into victories. When you lift your voice in worship, your barriers crumble. Mountains of fear, walls of doubt, and chains of oppression cannot stand in the presence of a heart overflowing with praise. It's praise that defeats the enemy, releases favor, and ushers in breakthroughs.

Choose to praise God even when the battle is fierce. Let your song of faith rise above the noise of discouragement. Trust that every enemy, every limitation, and every barrier is powerless against the sound of your praise. Raise your voice. Worship in spirit and truth. Watch the impossible fall. When the people shouted unto God, those walls came down and gave way to the power of God. Great power and unlimited strength is at your disposal when you shout praises to God. The same supernatural power that raised Jesus from the dead will tear down walls that stand before you. As you praise God wholeheartedly in faith, His power will be released and the obstacles in your life will fall down in front of you. Begin to shout and praise God with a voice of triumph because you know who you are in Christ. Praise God even when those walls are still standing. Then stand back and watch God work. Before long, those walls will be no more.

Even though the battle is raging in front of you, shout anyway! Declare the victory! Shout first and the victory will follow. It's good to get loud because the victory is tied to the intensity of your praise. Joshua said to the people, "Shout, for the Lord has given you the city!" (Josh. 6:16). The victory wasn't in the walls falling, the trumpets, or even the march - it was in the intensity of their obedience and praise. God often ties the breakthrough to the boldness of your worship. When you lift your voice, shout, and declare His goodness with passion, you release the power of heaven into your circumstances. Your loud praise becomes a spiritual weapon, aligning heaven and earth to bring the victory that God has already promised. Don't whisper when you should roar. Don't hold back when God is ready to move. Get loud! Let your praise be intense, unwavering, and fearless. The walls in your life - whatever seems impossible - will fall, because the Lord has already given you the victory. Shout it. Believe it. Receive it.

The people's shout was a celebration of the victory that would soon be theirs. There is incredible power in speaking your faith aloud. When you vocalize your celebration - your joy, your gratitude, your expectation of what God will do - you are not just expressing hope; you are activating your faith. Celebrate and watch God work. Celebrate the victories you have yet to see. Declare the breakthroughs that feel impossible. Lift your voice in joy over the promises of God. As you celebrate, you make room for God to move. Watch Him work for miracles have a way of answering your celebration. The problem is that too many people celebrate the wrong things. They celebrate the problem instead of the promise. For example, ten of the twelve spies celebrated the size of the giants that were in the Promised Land. But Caleb said, "Let us go up at once, and possess it; for we are well able to overcome it" (Num. 13:30). You don't deny the problem; you just don't celebrate the problem.

God likes it when you get loud because shouting will build up your faith. Every loud "Hallelujah!" and every bold cry of faith strengthens your spirit, pushes back doubt, and aligns your heart with His power. Don't whisper your victories - proclaim them! When you lift your voice, you aren't just speaking words; you're stirring heaven and building a faith that cannot be shaken. Let your shouts rise, for God sees them, rejoices in them, and answers them! Heb. 11:30 says, "By faith the walls of Jericho fell down after they were encircled for seven days." The people's shout was a shout of faith, and this is what caused the hand of God to move. Shout in faith in spite of what you're going through. When you do that, you make a declaration that the battle has already been won. It's a declaration that God is true to His Word, that He'll fulfill the promises He makes to you. It's a declaration that you believe His Word more than you believe your worries. That's what the shout declares.

The heart of a conqueror knows that a shout of praise can win a battle before it even begins. A true conqueror understands that victory begins in the heart before it ever appears on the battlefield. The heart of a conqueror knows that faith is not silent - it shouts. It knows that a shout of praise can move mountains, break chains, and cause the enemy to flee before the fight even begins. The people didn't need a sword or a spear or a battering ram. All they needed was a shout! Vocalize your faith! Vocalize your praise! Shout out loud and say, "God, I believe You for the victory!" When you lift your voice in worship, declaring the goodness and power of God, you are not just expressing gratitude - you are wielding a spiritual weapon. Your praise aligns heaven with your circumstance, stirring divine intervention in ways the human eye cannot see. Remember that battles are often won not by the strength of the hand, but by the faith in the heart. Let your praise be loud, unwavering, and full of confidence.

Praise brings God's presence into your situation. Ps. 22:3 says, "You inhabit the praises of Israel." The more time you spend in the presence of God, the more His power becomes visible in your life. When you pause to pray, worship, and meditate on His Word, you are not just filling your moments with devotion - you are opening your heart to divine movement. Just as the sun gradually illuminates the darkest corners, God's presence begins to shine in areas of your life that feel stagnant or impossible. You prepare the way to victory by giving praise to God. It was praise that brought the walls of Jericho down. Fill your home and your car with praise music. Ps. 50:23 says, "Whoever offers praise glorifies Me." Ps. 34:1 says, "I will bless the Lord at all times; His praise shall continually be in my mouth." Vs. 3, "Oh magnify the Lord with me, and let us exalt His name together." Magnifying God makes Him bigger than your problems. When God gets big, your problems get small. Praising God works.

| 13 |

"THE AGONY OF DEFEAT"

Many people visit their Promised Land but they don't live there. Why is that? Because there are principles you have to apply to your life, and most people don't do that. Every man comes to a crossroads - one that cannot be avoided, postponed, or ignored. It is the daily question that shapes our destiny: "Will we follow God's principles, or won't we? God never forces a man to walk in His ways. He invites. He calls. He beckons with wisdom, truth, and life. His principles are not chains - they are pathways to freedom, clarity, and blessing. They protect the heart, elevate the mind, and strengthen the spirit. They lead a man toward purpose, stability, and eternal reward. But every man must choose. Some choose convenience over commitment. Others choose the applause of people over the approval of God. Some prefer comfort to character, momentary pleasure to eternal promise. Yet the consequences of those choices always reveal themselves.

Joshua said it best, "Choose this day whom you will serve" (Josh. 24:15). That choice still stands before every man.

Not just once in life, but again and again in the quiet places of the heart - when no one sees, no one applauds, and no one pressures. The man who chooses God's principles may not always take the easiest road, but he will always take the right one. He will grow strong, lead well, and finish with honor because he built his life on the rock that cannot be shaken. Choose God's way. Choose God's truth. Choose God's principles today, tomorrow, and every day. The strength of your future begins with the choice you make right now. It's been said, "We are born looking like our parents, we die looking like our decisions." Every day is filled with decisions that have to be made. Deut. 30:15,19 (NLT) says, "Today I am giving you a choice between life and death, between prosperity and disaster. Oh, that you would choose life!'

Joshua 7 talks about a man who made a devastating choice. His name is Achan and in Hebrew his name means "trouble." He was a man who brought trouble into his life, the lives of his family, and the lives of the children of Israel. He did something so horrible that his life serves as a warning to what happens when we disobey God and do things our own way. God is a God who is "Holy, holy, holy" (Rev. 4:8). He is a God who hates sin and we forget that sometimes. God hates sin so much that He brings judgment on those who sin and don't repent of it. Sin is not a small matter to God. It is not a weakness to be overlooked, nor a flaw to be excused. Sin is rebellion against His holiness, an offense against His love, and a direct contradiction of everything He created us to be. Because God is perfectly righteous, He cannot ignore sin. Because He is perfectly just, He must confront it. And because He is perfectly loving, He warns us again and again so that we will turn and live.

Throughout Scripture, we see a consistent pattern: where there is unrepentant sin, there is always inevitable judgment. God judged the world in Noah's day, not because He delighted in destruction, but because mankind had filled the earth with violence and corruption. He judged Sodom, not out of cruelty, but because evil had consumed the people until there was no repentance left in them. Even His own people, Israel, faced judgment when they hardened their hearts and refused to turn from their wicked ways. But here is the mercy of God: He warns before He judges. He calls before He confronts. He pleads before He punishes. No loving Father will stand by and watch His children destroy themselves without intervening. Judgment is never God's first move - it is His last resort when humanity refuses His hand of mercy. His discipline is not meant to condemn us but to save us. The message is clear: Repent while there is time. Turn before judgment comes. Return to the God who longs to forgive.

Achan's story teaches us to fear God and stay clear of sin. Look at sin like a rattlesnake in the grass. You don't get close to it but stay as far away from it as you can. Sin always presents itself as harmless - quiet, subtle, almost friendly. But like a snake hidden in the grass, it waits for the perfect moment to strike. What begins as a small compromise soon grows into a deadly trap. Sin never bites lightly. Its venom spreads - slowly at first, then quickly - poisoning your peace, your joy, your relationships, and eventually your destiny. Just as a snake bite brings pain, infection, and sometimes death, sin brings consequences that no one can escape. The Bible says, "Be sure your sin will find you out" (Num. 32:23). God is loving, but He is also holy. And when we play with sin, we invite His correction and even judgment into our lives. Not because He wants to punish us, but because He wants to save us from destruction. God never warns us to take away our joy - He warns us to protect our lives.

The serpent in the Garden of Eden came with a lie and sin still speaks the same way today. But the truth is this: what you tolerate will eventually dominate. What you play with will eventually bite you and if not dealt with can turn deadly. The problem today is people in the church have lost their fear of God. They sin far too often and too easily. The story of Achan is written as an example for us living today. Before the walls of Jericho came down, some important commands were given. Josh. 6:17-19 says, "Jericho and everything in it must be completely destroyed as an offering to the Lord. Only Rahab the harlot shall live, she and all who are in their house. Be careful that you don't covet anything in it and take something that's cursed, endangering the camp of Israel with the curse and making trouble for everyone. Everything made from silver, gold, bronze, or iron is sacred to the Lord and must be brought into His treasury." God made it very clear. Everything in Jericho belonged to Him.

Joshua 6 ended on a high note, "So the Lord was with Joshua, and his fame spread throughout all the country" (vs. 27). Notice carefully that the next chapter begins with the word

"But..." Josh. 7:1 says, "But the children of Israel committed a trespass regarding the accursed things." The Bible then tells what that trespass was. It says a man named Achan "took of the accursed things; so that the anger of the Lord burned against the children of Israel" (vs. 1). This was a serious, serious sin. So bad was this sin that the anger of the Lord burned against what happened. This is not a light statement. Scripture records it with weight, intensity, and holy seriousness. Achan's disobedience wasn't merely a personal lapse in judgment - it was a deliberate violation of God's command, a sin that poisoned the camp and brought defeat to an entire nation. Achan acted in secret, but nothing is hidden from the sight of God. The things he took - things God had clearly forbidden - were not only stolen; they were under a curse.

When Achan touched what God called unclean, he stepped outside the boundaries of divine protection and into the territory of judgment. The gravity of this moment teaches us a sobering truth: private sin always has public consequences. Achan's actions affected not just himself, but his family, his tribe, and the entire nation of Israel. One man's compromise opened the door for defeat, discouragement, and confusion among the people of God. Why was God's anger so fierce? Because God is holy. Because God had spoken clearly. Because sin always destroys what God wants to bless. Achan's choice was a direct challenge to God's authority, and it revealed a heart willing to value forbidden treasure above obedience. Achan teaches us that it is never worth taking what God has forbidden. The shiny things of this world - riches, recognition, secret pleasures - promise gain but end in ruin. The "accursed things" may look appealing, but they carry spiritual weight greater than we can bear.

Why did the people have to give everything back to God? Joshua and all the people of Israel at that time were living under the Mosaic Law. Under the Mosaic law, you give back a portion of what God has given you in recognition that it all came from Him. Ex. 34:19 (NIV), "The first offspring of every womb belongs to Me, including all the firstborn males of your livestock." Ex. 34:26 (ESV), "The best of the firstfruits of your ground you shall bring to the house of the Lord your God." Prov. 3:9 (ESV), "Honor the Lord with your wealth and with the firstfruits of all your produce." This is the Mosaic Law of Firstfruits. Jericho was the first city they came to and everything in it belonged to the Lord. The people couldn't take one thing in Jericho and claim it as their own. Not one thing! If they give God His portion, they will be undefeated in the battles they fight. If not, they shall fall in ruin, and calamity will hunt them down. Their defeat will be swift, and destruction will follow close upon their heels.

Not knowing what Achan had done, Joshua sent spies to the next city they were to conquer, a small place called Ai. The spies returned and said only a few men would be needed to defeat this small village. "So about three thousand warriors were sent, but they were soundly defeated" (vs. 4). Thirty-six men were killed in this battle and vs. 5 says, "The Israelites were paralyzed with fear at this turn of events, and their courage melted away." What did Joshua do? He tore his clothes and fell facedown to the ground before the ark of the Lord, remaining there until evening (vs. 6). Joshua is experiencing the agony of defeat and he's having a meltdown. He asked God, "Why have You brought the people over the Jordan River only to have them get defeated at Ai?" (vs. 7). Joshua is a great warrior, a great man of faith, but right here he is questioning the character of God. Why? Because he doesn't understand how Israel got defeated by the small village of Ai.

Joshua now believes the camp of Israel will be defeated by all their enemies in the Promised Land (vs. 9). In a sense, He is blaming God for what happened. What does God do? He tells Joshua, "Get up! Why are you lying on your face like this?" (vs. 10). God tells Joshua to stand up and then proceeds to tell him what happened. "Israel has sinned and broken My covenant! They have stolen some the things that I commanded must be set apart for Me" (vs. 11). God is saying, "The problem is not with Me, it's with you and the people of Israel." There are moments when God calls His people to pause, look inward, and examine the condition of the heart. Joshua 7:11 is one of those moments. Israel had just seen the mighty walls of Jericho fall by the hand of God. Victory was fresh. Faith was high. Yet even in the glow of triumph, hidden disobedience was at work. God's words to Joshua cut straight to the heart: "Israel has sinned. They have taken what belongs to Me."

This is more than a story about one man's failure - it's a lesson for every believer. Sometimes we experience defeat, setbacks, or confusion not because God is distant, but because something in our lives is claiming what belongs to Him. What have we set our hands on that God has set apart for Himself? Time that should have been devoted to Him? Worship given to other pursuits? Resources used for self while neglecting the kingdom? Areas of compromise tucked away where no one sees? Achan hid what he took, thinking it would never be found out. But nothing hidden from God stays hidden for long. Not because He wants to condemn us but because He longs to restore us. Joshua 7 reminds us that God deals with sin not to destroy His people but to purify them, to bring them back under the shelter of His blessing. He wants us to walk in victory, but victory is impossible when disobedience is buried beneath the surface.

The good news is that confession restores what sin tries to steal. When we surrender what we've tried to hold back, grace floods in. God's presence returns. Strength rises again. The path forward becomes clear. When we set apart for God what He has claimed, we will once again walk in the fullness of His favor and the victory He intends for His people. Remember this about God: He is always good, loving, perfect, faithful, and true. Always! He is "merciful and gracious, longsuffering, and abounding in goodness and truth" (Ex. 34:6). Ps. 86:5 says, "For You, Lord, are good, and ready to forgive, and abundant in mercy to all those who call upon You." To walk in victory, your heart must be founded on the character of God. Victory is not measured by the absence of battles, but by the confidence you carry into them. And that confidence only comes from knowing who God is and not just what He does.

Too often, when life hits hard and circumstances make no sense, our emotions try to preach a false gospel. They whisper that God has forgotten us, abandoned us, or changed His mind. But the truth is this: the problem is never with God. His character is flawless. His nature is unchanging. His love, His wisdom, and His faithfulness stand unmoved by the storms that shake our world. Walking in victory means refusing to interpret God through the lens of your circumstances. Instead, interpret your circumstances through the lens of God's character. If He is good - and He is - then even what you don't understand is being woven into purpose. If He is faithful - and He is - then no setback can cancel His promise. If He is sovereign - and He is - then nothing enters your life without passing through His wise and loving hands. When you anchor your heart to His character, confusion cannot control you, disappointment cannot define you, and fear cannot defeat you.

Notice also that Joshua did not pray or seek God before he sent his men to Ai. They knew they needed God to beat Jericho, but not Ai. They thought they could defeat this tiny village on their own without God's help or input. Problems come when we don't think we need God's help. Joshua prayed about Jericho and won a great victory. He didn't pray over Ai and was soundly defeated. Setbacks often erupt without warning not because the enemy is strong, but because we forget where our strength comes from. The danger is not in the size of the battle but in fighting it without God. We don't fall because the obstacle is great. We stumble when we assume we can handle this on our own. We get in trouble when prayer is optional, when dependence becomes inconvenient, and when we lean on yesterday's victory instead of today's presence. Every Jericho-sized breakthrough begins with prayer. Every Ai-sized failure begins with self-reliance.

God wants to help us not just in the big battles, but in the small ones too. The truth is, there are no small battles. Each one requires His wisdom, His strength, and His guiding hand. We need God's help in everything we do, even the small, insignificant things. Say to God, "Show me! Tell me! Help me!" Seek Him out. Ask Him. Bring every decision to Him. Depend on Him daily, continually, humbly. Joshua was a praying man, but he didn't pray this time. If he did, God would have told him there was sin in the camp and thirty-six men would not have lost their lives. Joshua did pray after the defeat at Ai and God answered him. He said there was sin in the camp that had to be taken care of. He said some people had stolen the things that were set apart for Him. "And they have not only stolen them, but they have lied about it and hidden the things among their own belongings" (vs. 11). Somebody in the camp of Israel violated the Law of Firstfruits and God is about to reveal who that somebody is.

The people were to consecrate themselves, and then the following morning the perpetrator would be identified by lot. Prov. 16:33 says, "The lot is cast into the lap, but its every decision is from the Lord." When morning came, each tribe presented itself and the tribe of Judah was chosen by lot. Each family in the tribe was called out until finally it was revealed that Achan was the man who had sinned and brought great trouble to Israel. Joshua said to him, "My son, give glory to the Lord, the God of Israel, and honor Him. Tell me what you have done; do not hide it from me" (Josh. 7:19). Achan confessed his sin, admitting in Jericho he saw a robe, two hundred shekels of silver and a fifty-shekel bar of gold. He then said, "I coveted them and took them. And there they are, hidden in the earth in the midst of my tent, with the silver under it" (vs. 21). Messengers from Joshua confirmed the plunder was found in Achan's tent and brought it before the assembly.

The Israelites then stoned Achan, his family, and his livestock and burned their bodies. They also burned his tent, the plunder he had taken, and all that he had (vs. 25). They then raised over him a great heap of stones as a reminder of the high cost of disobeying God (vs. 26). The story of Achan is a stark reminder of the penalty of sin, which is death (Rom. 6:23). Achan's sin was serious. He took what belonged to God. The Israelites had been specifically warned about the consequences of not doing as God instructed. Achan's sin was a clear and willful violation of a direct order from God, and he did bring trouble to the entire camp of Israel. Also, he was given time to repent on his own. He could have come forward at any time but chose to wait as the lots were being cast. Rather than admit his guilt and call on the mercy of God, he instead tried to hide what he had done. Achan's sin found him out and he paid a heavy price for what he did. May his story be a warning to all of us.

| 14 |

"THOU SHALL NOT COVET"

The Tenth Commandment says, "Thou shall not covet" (Ex. 20:17). This is the only commandment that deals with the inner man. It was given to regulate your thoughts and how you think. James 1:15 reminds us that sin does not come from the outside world but begins deep within the heart of a person. Your inner thoughts, desires, and cravings can become the breeding ground for sin if left unchecked. Coveting is a serious sin because it brings forth destruction. It can lead to adultery, stealing, lying, and murder. That restless longing to take away and own something that belongs to another person is the spark that can ignite a host of sinful actions. It is the forerunner of all manner of sin and begins as a subtle thought, a quiet dissatisfaction, but if nourished, it grows into anger, deceit, jealousy, and every manner of wrongdoing. The word "covet" means 'to lust after; to long for with great desire; to take pleasure in the things God says "no" to.

Jesus said in Luke 12:15 (NLT), "Beware! Guard against every kind of greed. Life is not measured by how much you own." This is a call to examine what truly defines our lives. Too often, we are tempted to measure success by possessions, wealth, or status, but Jesus reminds us that these things cannot satisfy the soul. True life is found in love, faith, generosity, and the impact we have on others. Greed distracts us from what is eternal and steals our joy in the present. Guard your heart against the desire for more and instead seek God's kingdom and His righteousness. When you focus on spiritual riches - kindness, compassion, wisdom, and faith - your life will overflow with a peace and fulfillment that money can never buy. Remember, life is measured not by what you have, but by who you are in Christ and how you live for others. Let gratitude, contentment, and generosity be your true wealth for they endure far beyond material gain and enrich not only your life but the lives of those around you.

Achan's problem didn't start when he stole the accursed things, it started when he coveted. When he admitted his sin, Achan said, "I coveted them, and took them" (Josh. 7:21). The NLT says, "I wanted them so much that I took them." His coveting caused him to steal that which belonged to God. Beware of the sin of coveting, of wanting things God says you can't have. James 1:14,15 says, "But each one is tempted when he is carried away and enticed by his own lust. Then when lust has conceived it gives birth to sin; and when sin is full-grown, it brings forth death." These two verses offer a clear and sobering insight into the process of sin. Temptation does not come from God, but from within us, from our own desires and inclinations. Each of us faces moments when our lusts, cravings, or selfish ambitions quietly tug at our hearts. It starts small, often disguised as something harmless, yet it is in these moments that vigilance is crucial.

James teaches us that temptation, if entertained, grows. Lust is not just desire - it is desire acted upon or nurtured. When we dwell on it, it "conceives," and sin is born. Sin, when allowed to mature unchecked, leads to death - not just physical death, but spiritual death, separation from God, and the decay of our soul's well-being. At its root, coveting is the result of envy, a sin which, once it has taken root in the heart, leads to worse sin. Envy goes beyond casting a longing glare at something your neighbor owns. Once dwelled upon, envy of your neighbor's possessions can turn to feelings of resentment and hatred for the neighbor himself. This can turn into resentment toward God because He hasn't given you what your neighbor has. At its very core, envy is the love of self. Selfish people are always unhappy and discontented. The New Testament identifies covetousness as a form of idolatry, a sin that God detests (Col. 3:5).

Achan's problem was he didn't guard his heart against the sin of coveting. Prov. 4:23 says, "Guard your heart with all diligence, for out of it spring the issues of life." Where does coveting begin? It doesn't start with a word spoken or an action taken. It begins quietly in the heart. A glance lingers, a thought entertains what belongs to another, and slowly, desire takes root. Before long, the heart longs for what God has not given, and discontentment grows. When the heart craves what is not ours, it opens the door to envy, strife, and disobedience. It's been said that the eyes see what the heart desires. Achan said in Josh. 7:21, "Among the plunder I saw a beautiful robe from Babylon, two hundred silver coins, and a bar of gold weighing more than a pound." This just wasn't just a passing glance. Achan did not merely see these treasures. He stared at them. He looked at them with careful consideration. They filled his vision, dominated his thoughts, and captivated his heart.

This teaches us a crucial lesson that sin often begins with what we fixate on. It's not just the act of taking or doing wrong that corrupts us; it is the lingering gaze, the unchecked desire, the moment we let something earthly capture our attention more than God. When Eve saw that the forbidden fruit was good for food, that it was pleasant to the eyes, and a tree desirable to make one wise, she took its fruit and ate (Gen. 3:6). Eve saw the fruit, she coveted it, and she ate it. In 2 Sam. 11, David saw Bathsheba bathing and his heart and mind was filled with lust. He coveted her and laid down with her. Jesus said in Matt. 6:22,23, "Your eye is like a lamp that provides light for your body. When your eye is healthy, your whole body is filled with light. But when your eye is unhealthy, your whole body is filled with darkness." What do you see? What are you looking at? Achan was looking at something that wasn't his, something he couldn't have.

When your eyes and hearts dwell too long on what is forbidden, what is flashy, or what promises pleasure apart from God, you open the door to disobedience. Guard what you look at and guard your thoughts. The things you dwell on in your mind and heart shape the actions you take. Let your eyes and heart be captivated by God's glory, not the glitter of earthly gain. Do not let fleeting temptation dominate your vision and lead you into ruin. It's true, what you desire will eventually control you. Be careful what your heart clings to, for your deepest desires have the power to shape your life. If you desire worldly success, comfort, or approval above all else, those desires may become your master, guiding your decisions and pulling your spirit away from God's purpose. But when your desires are aligned with the will of God - love, faith, mercy, and truth - they guide you toward freedom, peace, and eternal joy. Remember, whatever you feed, you follow. Whatever you chase, you serve.

Guard your heart and let your desires be shaped by what is holy, for only then will your passions serve you, rather than enslave you. This must be done because when you desire something so much, you give it authority in your life. It will rule your heart and govern your life. Achan knew what he was doing was wrong, but he didn't care. His wrong desires caused him to sin anyway. Mark 4:19 says, "The deceitfulness of wealth and the desire for other things come in and choke the Word, making it unfruitful." Wrong desires is a sleeping wolf in the life of every person. With irresistible power, desire seizes mastery over the flesh. When wrong desires run rampant in your life, you lose the ability to think straight. All at once a smoldering fire is kindled. The flesh burns and is in flames. At this moment, you lose all reality of God in your life. Satan does not try to get you to hate God, he tries to get you to forget God. What you look at, and desire continually diminishes your spiritual desire for God.

Beware of the sin of covering. It is the sin of deception. Concerning the accursed things, Achan said, "I coveted them and took them; and behold, they are concealed in the earth inside my tent." (Josh. 7:21). He thought no one was watching but God saw it all. He sees everything we try to hide. Prov. 15:3, "The eyes of the Lord are in every place, keeping watch on the evil and the good." There is nothing hidden from the eyes of God. He sees it all - everything you do, everything you think, every desire that stirs within your heart. Nothing escapes His gaze, not the quiet struggles you keep to yourself, nor the secret joys you carry. Yet, this is not a cause for fear - it is a source of comfort. God knows you completely and you are fully embraced with His love. His sight is not judgment alone but understanding. Every longing, every prayer, every tear is known to Him, and nothing is wasted in His eyes. Seek His guidance in every thought and action and allow His wisdom to shape your desires.

The God who sees all is also the God who provides, protects, and perfects all that concerns you. Live with courage and integrity knowing that your life is fully seen by God. He even knows what's in your heart. 1 Sam. 16:7, "For the Lord does not see as man sees; for man looks at the outward appearance, but the Lord looks at the heart." God sees what truly matters: the intentions, the character, the integrity, and the faithfulness of the heart. What may appear weak, insignificant, or unremarkable to the world can be precious in God's eyes. The Lord is not impressed by status, beauty, or accolades. He cherishes a humble, faithful, and loving heart. Let your heart be open to Him today and allow His eyes to guide yours. Just know that He won't bless your life if there is hidden sin in your heart. Ps. 66:18, "If I regard iniquity in my heart, the Lord will not hear." The defeat at Ai was their only defeat in the Promised Land and it happened because of a hidden sin.

1 John 1:6 says, "If we say that we have fellowship with Him and yet walk in the darkness, we lie and do not practice the truth." This verse reminds us that claiming to have a relationship with God is not enough - our lives must reflect it. Fellowship with God is not just a label or a feeling; it is an active, daily commitment to walk in His light. Darkness represents sin, deception, or ignoring God's ways. When we continue in darkness while claiming closeness with God, we are living in contradiction, and our words become hollow. Walking in the light requires honesty, repentance, and obedience. It means confronting your weaknesses, turning away from sin, and aligning your actions with God's truth. It also means letting His Word guide your thoughts, words, and deeds, so that your fellowship with Him is visible not just in your heart but in our life. When you choose to walk in His light, your fellowship with Him is real, your life bears witness to the truth, and you become a reflection of His love in the world.

Achan hid the accursed things and acted like everything was okay. The truth is, it wasn't okay. He sinned and it affected his family and the entire camp of Israel. Know for sure that God will uncover all hidden sin. This is why you need to get sin out of the shadows and under the blood of Jesus. David's words in Psalm 32:5 remind us of the freedom and peace that come through honest confession. He said, "I acknowledged my sin to

You and my iniquity I have not hidden. I said, 'I will confess my transgressions to the Lord,' and You forgave the iniquity of my sin." Notice the pattern here: acknowledgment, confession, and forgiveness. David did not try to hide his sin or justify it - he brought it openly before God. That transparency opened the door to divine forgiveness and restoration. This teaches us that true spiritual healing begins with honesty before God. No matter the weight of guilt or shame we carry, God invites us to confess, not to condemn us, but to cleanse us.

When we admit our shortcomings, we release the burden of secrecy and receive the grace that only He can give. Let this verse encourage you: hiding sin leads to heaviness, but confessing it to the Lord brings freedom, peace, and a restored heart. Just as David experienced forgiveness, so too can you walk in the joy of God's mercy when you approach Him with a contrite heart. Prov. 28:13, "He who covers his sins will not prosper, but whoever confesses and forsakes them will have mercy." This verse reminds us that hiding our wrongs, trying to excuse or ignore them, only leads to stagnation and spiritual poverty. True prosperity - peace, freedom, and favor - comes when we are willing to face our sins honestly. Confession is not just admitting wrongdoing; it is acknowledging our need for God's guidance and His cleansing power. Forsaking sin means turning away from it, choosing a new path aligned with God's will. When we take these steps, mercy flows—not just forgiveness, but God's favor, protection, and restoration.

You must also be aware of the sin of squandering. This is the sin of not taking advantage of the opportunity you have to get things right with God. He told Joshua how to identify the man who had sinned. Tribe by tribe and family by family had to pass before him. Doing all this took time. Why did God do it this way? He was giving Achan the opportunity to get right, an opportunity to repent. God is gracious. His love is immeasurable, reaching farther than we can see, deeper than we can comprehend. He is not a distant judge waiting to condemn, but a loving Savior, ready to embrace us with open arms. Even when we stumble, even when we fall into sin, He does not turn away. Instead, He offers forgiveness, mercy, and restoration. His grace is patient. He gives us time and the opportunity to repent, to turn from what is wrong and walk in His ways. Speaking of Jezebel, God said in Rev. 2:21, "And I gave her time to repent of her sexual immorality, and she did not repent."

Ps. 130:3,4 says, "Lord, if you keep a record of our sins, who, O Lord, could ever survive? But you offer forgiveness, that we might learn to fear You." God calls us back to Himself not with anger, but with love, saying, "Come to Me, all who are weary, and I will give you rest" (Matt. 11:28). No matter how heavy your burden, no matter how far you feel from Him, His heart is ready to forgive. God's grace is not earned - it is freely given to all who humble themselves, to all who seek Him, and to all who desire to be made whole. Take hold of His forgiveness today. Let His love wash over your soul. Let the Savior who died for your sins show you the depths of His mercy. He is gracious. He is loving. He is your God. Achan was cornered into admitting his sin, but he never confessed and repented of it. He wasn't sorry he sinned; he was sorry he got caught. Achan squandered this opportunity that was given to him. He was guilty of the sin of coveting, guilty of the sin of covering, and guilty of the sin of squandering.

Achan and his family were stoned to death and then their bodies were burned with fire. The point being, God will judge sin! He patiently calls people to repentance, warning that judgment is real and inevitable. Those who reject His ways will face His righteous judgment, for He cannot ignore sin. Lev. 10:1 says Nadab and Abihu, the sons of Aaron, offered profane fire before the Lord which He had not commanded them. Look what happens next. Vs. 2 says, "So fire went out before the Lord and devoured them, and they died before the Lord." In the New Testament, Ananias and Sapphira lied to the Holy Spirit, and both fell over dead on the spot (Acts 5). Don't lose sight of the holiness of God. He hates sin and you should too. God is holy, perfect in righteousness, pure in every way, and utterly opposed to sin. His holiness is not just an attribute; it is a standard, a call, and a warning. When we forget His holiness, we risk becoming comfortable with compromise, numb to sin, and blind to the danger it brings to our souls.

God hates sin because it destroys, deceives, and separates us from Him. As His followers, we are called not only to recognize sin for what it is but also to hate it in our own lives. Reject temptation, guard your heart, and pursue righteousness with unwavering devotion. Remember, holiness is not about perfection in yourself - it's about reflecting the purity and character of God. Stay close to Him, honor Him in every thought and action, and let the fear of sin drive you toward His grace. Don't lose sight of God's holiness, for it is the light that guides you, protects you, and calls you higher. Prov. 8:13 says, "The fear of the Lord is to hate evil." If you say no to repenting of your sin, judgment will fall severely. Is.1:20 says, "If you refuse and rebel, you shall be devoured by the sword." Achan and his family were wiped out because they refused to repent. But those who turn to Him in humility, confessing their sins and seeking His forgiveness, will find grace, mercy, and restoration.

The word "repent" means 'a change of mind.' It means to change your thinking which, in turn, will change your behavior. Repentance is not saying you're sorry. People can say they're sorry all day long and not repent. They're sorry today but do the same thing tomorrow. Solomon tells us why this happens. Eccl. 8:11, "Because the sentence against an evil work is not executed speedily, therefore the heart of the sons of men is fully set in them to do evil." People think they're getting away with sin if God doesn't strike them down immediately. No, what you sow is what you reap (Gal. 6:7). Remember, judgment is coming but God's love is greater. He calls us now to live holy lives, to honor Him, and to be reconciled with Him before it is too late. Fear God for He is a consuming fire (Heb. 12:29). Sin cannot coexist with His perfection, and He will right every wrong. Obey what He tells you to do because "it is a fearful thing to fall into the hands of the living God" (Heb. 10:31).

| 15 |

"A NEW BEGINNING"

Israel had just been soundly defeated at Ai in their second battle in the Promised Land. This defeat did not happen because God had failed the people, it happened because the people failed God. It happened because there was sin in the camp. When the sin problem was done away with, it was time to turn defeat into victory. When we put our full faith in Jesus, we are forgiven of our sins (1 John 1:9). Because of what Jesus did on the cross, we can walk in victory day after day after day. At the cross, Jesus didn't just forgive sin - He removed its power to define us. The very thing that once separated us from God was stripped of its authority. And once the barrier was gone, heaven declared a new season: a season where shame gives way to confidence, weakness gives way to strength, and defeat is transformed into undeniable victory. Through Christ, we are no longer fighting for victory; we are fighting from victory. The enemy's greatest weapon - sin - has been crushed.

The people of God can now rise, not as victims of their past, but as conquerors through the One who loved them. When sin was dealt with, God opened the door for restoration, triumph, and purpose. The blood settled the issue; the resurrection sealed the outcome; and the Spirit empowers the walk. Now it's our turn to step forward and live in the victory that has already been won. Scottish theologian Alexander Whyte said, "The victorious Christian life is a series of new beginnings." Prov. 24:16, "For a righteous man may fall seven times and rise again." Each time you fall down and get back up, that's a new beginning. A righteous person isn't someone who never falls. A righteous person is someone who refuses to stay down. Rising is the evidence of God's grace working inside you. Getting up is your declaration that the story isn't over. Each new beginning is a sign that God's mercy is still flowing. Your scars become your testimony. Your setbacks become steppingstones to a better life.

Don't fear falling. Fear staying down. Your next beginning starts the moment you stand back up. Every time you rise, you rise stronger, wiser, and closer to the purpose God planted in you. The people of Israel fell in Josh. 7 but in Josh. 8 they get back up again. They're about to have a new beginning with God. Joshua is standing in front of a pile of stones that covered the bodies of Achan and his family. These stones represented God's judgment on sin in the camp of Israel. The people are still shaken up over what happened. Why wouldn't they be? Defeat in one's life often brings worry, intimidation, and loss of heart. But when we turn from our sins and return to the Lord, God brings great encouragement to replace the fear and discouragement. He lifts the head that has been hanging low. He strengthens the hands that have grown weak. His presence begins to push out fear, and His love begins to silence the discouragement that once tried to suffocate us.

Scripture shows this pattern again and again. When Israel returned to God, He sent His word to strengthen them. When the prodigal son came home, the father ran to him with restoration. When we draw near to God, He draws near to us - not with condemnation, but with comfort and courage. Repentance is not just turning away from sin - it's turning toward hope. It's turning toward the God who restores, renews, and revives. It's stepping out of darkness into the warmth of His grace. And with every step we take toward Him, His encouragement grows stronger than our fears, His promises louder than our doubts, and His peace deeper than our discouragement. If your heart feels heavy today, turn back to Him. Your return is the doorway to renewed strength. Your repentance is the pathway to divine encouragement. And your surrender is the place where fear loses its power and God's courage rises within you. He is waiting - not to rebuke you, but to restore you.

Josh. 8:1 says, "Then the Lord said to Joshua, 'Do not be afraid or discouraged.'" The Lord first encourages Joshua, and then He encourages the rest of the people. Vs. 1 continues, "Take all your fighting men and attack Ai, for I have given you the king of Ai, his people, his town, and his land." Notice God said to take all the men of war, not just three thousand like they did last time. This is a new beginning for the people of Israel and they're going to do things God's way, not their own. God wants you to not be afraid and discouraged and He wants you to re-attack the enemy that defeated you. The same God who stood with you in the valley is the God who empowers you to rise again. He does not call you to retreat - He calls you to re-attack, not in your own strength, but in His. Face the enemy that once defeated you with holy boldness. The enemy that once knocked you down will not win the second time, because this time you are walking with renewed strength, renewed faith, and renewed authority.

When God says, "Go again," He also guarantees, "You will not lose again." You can win this battle because in Christ you've been given the victory. However, a very important lesson is given here in Joshua 8. The people are about to learn that walking in victory after you sinned will be much more difficult than if you had obeyed God in the beginning. When we have sinned, the road back to victory can be very long and very demanding. For some people, it may take the rest of their lives to recover from what they did. That's just the plain, honest truth. The lesson here is it's better to obey God in the first place. Indeed, it's a hard road back to victory after the defeat of sin. At Jericho, the people obeyed God and won a great victory with very little work on their part. But now, after the defeat that sin brought into the camp, the road to victory is going to be laborious and very burdensome. God will still bring the victory but it's going to be far more strenuous and complicated than if they had obeyed God in the first place.

There are seasons in our lives when God, in His mercy, still brings us into victory even after we've taken the long road. He's faithful like that. He doesn't abandon us when we drift, delay, or detour. His purpose for our lives is bigger than our mistakes, and His love is stronger than our stubbornness. But the truth of the matter is that it's always more complicated when we don't follow God's way from the start. When we ignore His prompting, when we choose our own timing, when we rely on our own strength, we often end up fighting battles that were never meant to be battles at all. What should have been a straight path becomes a maze. What could have been simple becomes a struggle. Yes, God will still give you the victory, but it won't be as simple as it could have been. Now He must teach us, refine us, and correct us along the way. He takes the longer, harder road we created and still leads us to the place He intended for us all along.

Josh. 8:3 says Joshua called up thirty thousand of his best warriors instead of the three thousand he sent previously. To win this battle, it's going to take ten times more effort than it did the first time. Joshua has to devise an elaborate plan in order to draw the enemy out of their stronghold (vs. 4-6). They're going to pretend to run away to get the enemy to chase after them. Joshua says to the first group of warriors, "You will jump up from your ambush and take possession of the town, for the Lord God will give it to you." As this chapter continues, this elaborate and difficult plan for victory works, and all the army of Ai was drawn out by Joshua's tactics. Vs. 18,19, "Then the Lord said to Joshua, 'Point the spear in your hand toward Ai, for I will hand the town over to you.' Joshua did as he was commanded. As soon as Joshua gave this signal, all the men in ambush jumped up from their position and poured into the town. They quickly captured it and set it on fire."

Vs. 22 says the entire army of Ai was caught in the crossfire and not a single person survived. Vs. 27, "Only the livestock and the treasures of the town were not destroyed, for the Israelites kept these as plunder for themselves, as the Lord had commanded Joshua." If Achan would have only waited on the Lord, he would have had his portion of the plunder instead of being dead. Sin always speaks with urgency. It whispers, " Don't wait. Get what you can now." Sin always pushes you toward the shortcut - toward the easy path that costs far more than it promises. But God speaks differently. His voice is steady, sure, and full of love. He says, "Wait and I will give you all you need in due time. What I give will be right, complete, and without sorrow added to it." God never withholds anything good from His children. He simply gives it in the right season, when it will strengthen you rather than destroy you. His timing is perfect. His gifts are complete. And His plans for you are worth the wait.

Every time you choose to wait on the Lord, you are choosing faith over fear, trust over impulse, and destiny over distraction. Waiting is not punishment - it is positioning. God is aligning what you need, shaping who you are, and preparing a blessing that will not crumble under the weight of your future. Joshua hangs the king of Ai on a pole and at sunset buries him under a great pile of stones (vs. 29). This was a long and hard-fought battle for Israel as they returned to victory after their defeat at Ai. Making things right is always harder than if you had listened and obeyed in the first place. Obedience in the beginning is easier than repair in the end. Consider the long and hard road back from sin before you decide to choose sin. Allow this to motivate you to refuse sin and do it God's way to begin with. Disobedience may feel easy in the moment, but it always costs more in the end - more time, more tears, more effort, and sometimes more pain.

Christianity was never meant to be a passive walk but a powerful warfare. The moment you said yes to Jesus, you stepped onto a spiritual battlefield. Darkness pushes back against light. The enemy plots against every believer who dares to grow, advance, and stand firm in God's truth. This is why Scripture does not tell us to relax, hide, or retreat but to fight the good fight of faith (1 Tim. 6:12). God would never command you to fight if there were no war. The devil roams around like a roaring lion seeking whom he may devour (1 Peter 5:5). Walking in victory is not a walk in the park. It's going to be a battle. Every day, unseen forces wage war for your purpose, your peace, your mind, your family, and your destiny. The attacks may be subtle - discouragement, temptation, fear, confusion - or they may be fierce and overwhelming. The sad reality is most Christians are not experiencing the thrill of victory; they're experiencing the agony of defeat. They ask, "Where's the power? Where's the victory?"

Scripture tells you what's possible with God in terms of living in victory. At the same time, Phil. 2:12 says you need to "work out your own salvation with fear and trembling." In other words, you have to apply yourself to walk out the Christian life. Salvation is a gift freely given, purchased by the blood of Jesus, and offered to anyone who believes. But though salvation is a gift, spiritual maturity is a journey. Paul's words are not a call to earn what Christ has already paid for, but a call to cultivate what God has planted within you. When the Scripture says to "work out your own salvation," it means to bring to the surface what God has placed on the inside. It is like a miner digging out treasure that already exists beneath the ground. God has deposited His Spirit, His power, and His purpose within you. Now He invites you to cooperate with Him so that what is inward becomes visible outward. You are told to do this "with fear and trembling" - not with dread, but with deep reverence and dependence on God.

Treat your walk with Christ with holy seriousness. Every decision, every step, every choice matters because your life is meant to reflect the One who saved you. You "work it out" by yielding daily to God's Word, resisting the pull of sin, and allowing the Holy Spirit to shape your character. You "work it out" by fighting the good fight of faith when temptation presses in. You "work it out" by choosing obedience even when it's hard, inconvenient, or countercultural. This is not a lonely effort, for the very next verse says, "For it is God who works in you both to will and to do His good pleasure. You work out what God works in. Your part is surrender; His part is transformation. So walk with reverence. Live with intention. Guard your heart. Cultivate holiness. Pursue Christ with diligence and awe. God has begun a good work in you, and He will finish it as you faithfully work out what He has placed within you. Keep digging. Keep growing. Keep shining.

The book of Joshua shows you how to experience victory in your life for it teaches us that there are basic and essential principles to walking in victory. First, you must believe the truth concerning the character of God. A. W. Tozer said, "What you think of when you think about God is the most important thing about you." Your thoughts about God shape the very core of who you are. If your thoughts of Him are small, limited, or distant, your faith will reflect that. But if your thoughts of God are vast, loving, and mighty, they will shape your courage, your hope, and your perspective on life. The image you carry of God isn't just an idea - it is the lens through which you see the world, yourself, and your future. When you meditate on His goodness, His power, and His unfailing love, your life begins to align with those truths. Your thoughts of God are more than thoughts - they are the blueprint of your character, the compass for your choices, and the anchor of your soul.

Who God is in your mind becomes who you are in life. This is why you must believe James 1:17, "Every good gift and every perfect gift is from above and comes down from the Father of lights." James is saying God doesn't have a dark side. 1 John 1:5, "God is light, and in Him is no darkness at all." Down in your heart you've got to be convinced that you can trust God because He is always loving, kind, and perfect. Ps. 100:5 says, "For the Lord is good; His mercy and lovingkindness are everlasting, His faithfulness endures to all generations." The Lord is good, beyond measure, and His goodness shines even in our darkest moments. His mercy reaches far beyond what we can comprehend. Nothing happens to you until it first filters through the fingers of God. If you believe that, you can handle anything that comes your way. After the defeat at Ai, Joshua had a meltdown and forgot the character of God. He forgot that God is always faithful, He never makes a mistake, and He is always true to His Word.

Second, you must believe that praying to God comes with a promise. God said in Jer. 33:3, "Call to Me and I will answer you, and I will tell you great and mighty things which you do not know." This verse is a divine invitation to enter into a personal conversation with God. It reminds us that prayer is not just about asking; it's about reaching out with expectation, trust, and intimacy. When life feels uncertain, confusing, or overwhelming, this promise assures us that we are not left to navigate it alone. God is waiting to hear your voice, to respond, and to reveal His wisdom and plans that go beyond your understanding. It's been said that only desperate people pray. The people were desperate going up against Jericho. They weren't desperate when facing Ai. Not praying reveals a pride problem. The people didn't think they needed God's help defeating Ai. They could do it on their own, or so they thought. They didn't pray and got in trouble because of it.

Third, you must hear and take heed to the Word of God. To walk in victory, you've got to walk by faith and not by sight (2 Cor. 5:7). What is faith? Faith is an act of obedience. It's simply doing what God tells you to do. Walking by faith means taking steps even when the path is unclear, believing even when the situation looks hopeless, and trusting that God's plan is greater than any obstacle. Victory is not found in what you see, but in who you follow. Fix your eyes on Him, step forward in obedience, and watch as what seems impossible becomes your testimony. The world will often show you obstacles, challenges, and circumstances that seem impossible to overcome. Your eyes may tell you, "It's too hard," or "You can't do this." But faith sees beyond what the eyes can perceive - it looks to the promises of God and trusts in His power. Victory belongs to those who trust, not to those who merely look. When you do what God says, you'll experience victory (1 John 5:4).

Faith grows and is strengthened by declaring the Word of God. Speak out what you believe. Faith is not passive - it is alive, active, and grows when we give it voice. The Word of God is not just something to read; it is a seed planted in our hearts that flourishes when spoken. Every time you declare the promises of God over your life, you water that seed. Every time you speak His truth in the face of doubt or fear, your faith strengthens. At Jericho, Joshua told the people, "Shout, for the Lord has given you the city!" (Josh. 6:16). He was speaking out what he believed. Words carry power. They align your spirit with God's reality, not with the world's limitations. Your declarations shape your heart, fortify your faith, and release God's power into your life. Declare the Word of God over your life and do what it tells you to do. After the defeat at Ai, Joshua heard what God said and proceeded to deal with the sin of Achan. He did what God told him to do and shortly thereafter won the victory over Ai.

| 16 |

"ANGEL OF LIGHT"

To have the heart of a conqueror, you have to continually be seeking God. Opposition will come and you need to ask God what to do about it. You have a spiritual enemy who has schemes, plans, and devices to deceive you. Eph. 6:11 calls these "the wiles of the devil." He is not passive, not indifferent, and not idle. Scripture is very clear that his attacks are intentional. His strategies are calculated. His plans are designed with one purpose in mind: to deceive, discourage, and ultimately derail you from the destiny God has ordained for your life. The devil desires to infiltrate and bring compromise to damage and destroy your relationship with God. Sometimes the enemy comes at us like a deranged lion, full force and straight on like a freight train. And sometimes he comes in like a friend, subtly slipping into our lives to bring damage and destruction. He comes with subtle deceit, and his desire is to slip into your life and slowly destroy your relationship with God.

Don't get so confident in your ability to make your own decisions that you never go to God asking for His help. It's easy to take pride in your own abilities and decisions, to feel like you have everything under control. But no matter how strong, wise, or capable you are, you must never let your confidence replace your dependence on God. True strength comes not from self-reliance, but from recognizing that you need His guidance in every choice, big or small. When you stop seeking God's wisdom, you risk walking blind into mistakes, pride, and unnecessary struggles. God delights in guiding those who seek Him. Let your confidence in your abilities be matched by your faith in His wisdom. You don't know everything and see everything, but He does. Without God's help and direction, you might make decisions that will have a negative effect on your life for years to come. Sad to say, this is what happened in Joshua 9. The leaders of Israel are deceived by an enemy who came in looking like a friend.

Life is full of decisions that have to be made. Some are small while others shape the course of your entire life's journey. Each choice is an opportunity to exercise wisdom, faith, and discernment. Decisions are not just about outcomes; they reveal the condition of your heart. The Bible reminds us in Proverbs 3:5-6 to "Trust in the Lord with all your heart and lean not on your own understanding; in all your ways submit to Him, and He will make your paths straight." Give God complete confidence and reliance. Don't hold back; trust Him fully in every area of life. Human wisdom is limited. Don't rely only on your intellect or logic; God's perspective is higher and wiser. When faced with uncertainty, you are not alone - God is there to guide your steps. Decisions made in prayer and alignment with His Word bring peace, even when the path ahead seems unclear. Life may present several crossroads, but every choice can become a steppingstone toward growth, purpose, and blessing when you seek His will first.

In Joshua 9, Joshua and the leaders of Israel have to make a very important decision. A nation comes to them and wants to make a treaty with Israel. What should they do? What decision should they make? Vs. 1 says all the kings in the Promised Land heard what happened at Jericho and Ai. What did these kings do? "These kings combined their armies to fight as one against Joshua and the Israelites" (vs. 2). This is opposite of how they felt in Josh. 5:1, "Their hearts melted and they no longer had the courage to face the Israelites." What's the difference? Before Achan sinned, nobody wanted to fight the nation of Israel. But now, after Achan sinned, all the kings are bold and want to fight. If tiny Ai can beat Israel one time, they believe they can beat them also. Make no mistake about it. Sin has consequences that will affect your future. When sin is tolerated, it creates future battles that you wouldn't otherwise have to fight. These future battles will be harder to win, so don't play around with sin.

When you've had a great victory, be careful not to get spiritually arrogant or self-confident. Victory is sweet, and the joy of overcoming can fill your heart with confidence. But remember, the greatest victories are never achieved by your strength alone. When triumph comes, it's easy to let pride or self-reliance take root. The danger is not in the victory itself, but in what victory can quietly do to your spirit. Stay humble. Give God the glory. Let each success remind you of His power working through you, not your own. Spiritual arrogance can blind you to your need for continued growth, prayer, and dependence on the Lord. True strength comes from humility, and lasting victories are those that keep you close to God rather than lift you above Him. Rejoice in your victories but keep your heart soft, your hands lifted, and your eyes fixed on the One who makes all triumph possible because while you're celebrating, the enemy is still out there planning to take you out.

All the kings in the Promised Land joined forces to fight against Israel. All, that is, except one. After seeing what God had done for the Israelites so far, the enemy in Gibeon decided to take a different approach. Josh. 9:3,4 (NLT) says, "But when the people of Gibeon heard what Joshua had done to Jericho and Ai, they resorted to deception to save themselves." Instead of the "straight on" approach, they used the "subtle deception" approach which works just as well, if not better. Remember, the enemy is both a deranged lion and a subtle serpent. In fact, more times than not, he uses the subtle approach more than the straight on approach. Why? Because too often Christians think too highly of themselves. They fall into the trap of pride, believing they are too wise, too strong, or too faithful to be deceived by the enemy. They think there is no way the devil can get the best of them. They're not constantly fearful that this can happen to them. Yet, the truth is, it happens all the time.

Scripture reminds us that overconfidence can blind us to subtle lies and temptations. Just as Satan tempted even the most devout with subtle deceit, we too can be led astray when we think we are immune. Humility is our safeguard - acknowledging that apart from God's guidance, we are vulnerable. A heart that relies on God stays alert, discerning, and protected against the enemy's schemes. It is a heart that is alive and vigilant. When you depend on your own strength, you become blind to the subtle schemes of the enemy and vulnerable to deception. But when your trust is anchored in God, your heart is sharpened with discernment. You see clearly what is true, what is harmful, and what requires patience and wisdom. God's strength becomes your shield, His Spirit your guide, and His Word your safeguard. Such a heart does not stumble; it remains alert, protected, and steadfast, walking confidently in the path of righteousness while the enemy's plans are rendered powerless.

Josh. 9:4 says the nation of Gibeon "sent ambassadors to Joshua, loading their donkeys with weathered saddlebags and old, patched wineskins." Vs. 5, "They put on worn-out, patched sandals and ragged clothes. And the bread they took with them was dry and moldy." Lying, these men from Gibeon said, "We have come from a distant land to ask you to make a peace treaty with us." The nations in the promised land were larger and stronger than they were (Deut. 7:1) so when a nation comes to make peace with them is sounds very attractive. The Israelites replied, "How do we know you don't live nearby? For if you do, we cannot make a treaty with you" (vs. 7). They knew that Moses commanded no treaties were to be made in the Promised Land. The visitors replied, "We are your servants." Joshua asked, "Who are you, and where do you come from?" (vs. 8). Joshua only asked these two questions. He didn't investigate. He didn't think it over. Worse yet, he didn't pray about it.

Joshua is judging by appearances. Their clothes were torn, and their bread was moldy. Watch carefully because Joshua never gets an answer to these two questions. The people from Gibeon answered, "From a very far country your servants have come, because of the name of the Lord your God" (vs. 9). They didn't say who they were or specifically where they came from. They lied and said they were from a far country when they only lived twenty-five miles away. They then said, "For we have heard of His fame and all that He did in Egypt" (vs. 9). They're stroking the ego of the Israelites. They're saying, "We heard about you. You're famous." Because they heard what God did for them, they said their elders sent them to make a peace treaty with Israel (vs. 9-11). Remember, these people are the enemy, the very ones they were commanded to wipe out "lest they teach you to do according to all their abominations which they have done for their gods, and you sin against the Lord your God" (Deut. 20:18).

To deceive Joshua into thinking they've journeyed a long way, they pointed out how worn out their clothes were and how moldy their bread was (vs. 12,13). It is amazing the far extremes the enemy will go to in order to deceive the people of God and lead them down the dark path. He does not attack only at obvious points; his strategies are subtle, cunning, and relentless. The enemy is a master of disguise. He presents lies wrapped in the fabric of truth, temptation dressed in the garments of opportunity, and fear masked as wisdom so that what seems obvious may lead you astray. His goal is always the same: to lead God's children away from the light and down the dark path of destruction. The devil thrives in confusion, fear, and doubt. He seeks to cloud your mind, twist your thoughts, and make the path of righteousness seem heavy and burdensome. Sin, on the other hand, is shrouded in deception, appearing attractive and harmless, but it always leads to destruction.

Do not be fooled by sin's temporary allure. Notice carefully that the enemy here is masquerading as a friend. Grasp the shocking significance of 2 Cor. 11:14,15 that says, "Satan himself transforms himself into as angel of light. It is no wonder that his servants also disguise themselves as servants of righteousness." The devil doesn't always appear as the enemy we expect. Often, he cloaks himself in what seems pure, holy, or righteous to lure us into deception. His servants, too, adopt this strategy, presenting themselves as ministers of truth while hiding motives that lead away from God. The challenge for every believer is discernment. Not everything that glitters spiritually is genuine. True light aligns with God's Word, brings peace, humility, and holiness, and points to Jesus. Anything that distorts His truth, stirs pride, fear, or division, or glorifies self instead of God should raise a red flag. We are called to test the spirits (1 John 4:1) and to walk in the Spirit, guided by wisdom and truth.

These Gibeonites have gone to elaborate measures to look and act like a friend in order to gain Joshua's trust and get inside his life. They came in shabby clothes as a disguise. They approached Joshua as if they were weak, harmless, and seeking a covenant with Israel. Without seeking counsel of the Lord, Joshua believed the lies these people were telling him. Josh. 9:14, "So the men took some of their provision, but did not ask counsel from the Lord." This verse is a sobering reminder of how easy it is to act in haste without seeking God's guidance. The Israelites were about to make a critical decision - interacting with the Gibeonites - but instead of pausing to seek God's direction, they relied on their own judgment and immediate needs. They took some provisions, perhaps thinking it was harmless, but in doing so, they set themselves up for consequences they could have avoided. Spiritually, this teaches us that even seemingly small decisions must be filtered through God's wisdom.

Acting without consultation with the Lord may seem practical or urgent, but it can lead to compromise, deception, or missed blessings. God desires for us to bring all our plans, big and small, before Him. Vs. 15, "And Joshua made peace with them and made a covenant with them, to let them live, and the leaders of the congregation swore to them." This decision turned out to be a horrible mistake and many problems came as a result of this. Generations were affected by this one decision that was made without seeking the counsel of the Lord. The key lesson here is intentional dependence. Before you take action - especially in matters affecting your faith, integrity, or relationships - we must ask, "Lord, what is Your will in this situation?" Waiting for His guidance may feel inconvenient or slow, but it will protect you from making choices that may lead to regret. Seek God's counsel and do not fall into the trap of relying on our own understanding, no matter how pressing the situation may seem.

Don't make any decisions without first asking God what He wants you to do. Do this no matter how good the opportunity may appear to be. All the people of the Promised Land was against Israel yet here comes the Gibeonites saying they want to be their friends. What the Gideonites were offering the people of Israel appeared to be a good thing. Be careful about making quick decisions. Don't be fooled by outward appearances. You can't tell a book by its cover. What Joshua didn't know is that these people were from a country that wanted to attack and kill them. Be careful about making decisions when you don't have all the information. Don't make quick decisions only to find out it was the wrong decision. Slow down! Wait! You don't have enough information! You're about to make a big mistake! There's more to making a decision than meets the eye. Take time to research the matter. Pray and God will give you more than enough wisdom to make a good and wise decision."

Three days later, the children of Israel found out the Gibeonites were their neighbors and not people from a far-away land (vs. 16). It was now time for Israel to attack the cities these people came from, but they didn't do it because of the treaty they had made. The people of Israel didn't like this. Vs. 18 says, "Then all the congregation murmured against the leaders." Instantly there is disunity and frustration in the camp of Israel. There is a loss of influence the leaders have over the people. The people are not looking for performers; they are looking for shepherds. They are looking for voices that carry the breath of God. True leadership is not about position; it's about carrying the presence of God. When Moses came down from the mountain, his face shone. The people listened because they saw evidence of God on him. When David stepped onto the battlefield, he held no title, no armor, and no rank yet Israel followed him because they saw courage and faith burning in him.

Influence is not inherited; it is earned. And in many places today, we are witnessing a loss of influence among leaders - not because the people have changed, but because the character of leadership has shifted. Influence fades when conviction fades. Influence weakens when example weakens. Influence disappears when spiritual authority is replaced with personal ambition. If you want influence, spend time with the One who holds all power. If you want impact, let God shape your character. If you want the people to follow, learn first to follow Him. When leaders return to God, influence returns to leaders. God is not looking for perfect leaders - He is looking for surrendered ones. Leaders who return to prayer, who return to holiness, who return to compassion, who return to truth, will once again speak with weight, power, and spiritual authority. Jesus taught "as one having authority," and the crowds were drawn to Him because His life matched His words.

Then all the leaders said to the people, "We have sworn to them by the Lord God of Israel; now therefore we may not touch them. This is what we must do. We must let them live, for divine anger would come upon us if we broke our oath" (vs. 19,20). Israel was stuck. There is now nothing they can do. They cannot go back on the treaty or God will judge them. You say, "But they lied!" That's not how God sees it. God says, "You gave your word, now you must keep your word." Prov. 15:4 (NLT) says people must "keep their promises even when it hurts." This verse reminds us that words have power, and integrity matters deeply. Be aware, some decisions cannot be reversed. You've got to live with the decisions you make. Joshua and the leaders of Israel made a massive mistake. Their failure to seek God's counsel cost them a portion of their inheritance. God told them to take the land but now there are several cities they can't take because of this wrong decision.

Joshua let the Gibeonites live but made them slaves to the people of Israel. However, generations later they would cause problems for King Saul and King David. These problems would have been avoided if they had been wiped out like God first intended. But because of Joshua's mistake of not seeking God's counsel, the Gibeonites were spared and later became a thorn in Israel's flesh. Not consulting the Lord is a sure way for the schemes of the enemy to take up residence in your life. When you fail to seek the Lord's guidance, you leave doors open for the enemy's schemes to take root in your life. The Word reminds us that plans made apart from God are fragile and vulnerable, but those established with Him are fortified and blessed. Let God illuminate your path and expose any hidden snares. When God is at the center of your plans, no scheme of the enemy can take permanent residence in your life. Guard your heart with prayer and make His guidance your first and final step in every matter.

| 17 |

"BOLD PRAYERS"

Living in the Promised Land is a life of victorious spiritual warfare. You can't be a conqueror if you're always shrinking back when opposition comes your way. Victory was never meant for the timid, but for those who dare to stand their ground when the enemy pushes hardest. Every conqueror in Scripture - David, Joshua, Gideon, Paul - became who they were not because life was easy, but because when resistance came, they refused to retreat. Opposition is not a sign that you're failing; it's often proof that you're heading in the right direction. The enemy doesn't attack what isn't a threat. He rises against you because he sees the calling, the anointing, and the breakthrough that is ahead. This is why God commands you to be strong and courageous. When you become the man God wants you to be, there will be places and opportunities and problems that He will want you to conquer. You must declare all-out war against the enemy in order to take possession of the Promised Land.

In Christ you'll move from victory to victory over the enemy who stands against you and the life Jesus died to give you. To be victorious, conquerors must pray big prayers because they know they have a big God. When you believe God will do big things, you position your heart to see big things. Faith is not just hoping for the best - it is the confident expectation that God is who He says He is and will do what He promised. When you enlarge your belief, you enlarge the space for God to move. God honors bold faith. He responds to the heart that refuses to shrink back, the heart that says, "Lord, I don't know how, but I trust You." When you dare to believe beyond your ability, you invite God to work beyond your limitations. Open your eyes with faith. Lift your expectations higher. As you believe Him for greater things, you'll witness His power, His provision, and His faithfulness in ways you've never seen before. God moves mightily where hearts believe boldly.

Josh. 10:1-5 tells how the Canaanite king of Jerusalem became upset with the Gibeonites because they made peace with Israel. He gathered four other kings and set out to make war with Gibeon for their rebellion against the other Canaanite nations. This could have been a great opportunity for Joshua. He was supposed to wipe out Gibeon in the first place but couldn't do it because he was deceived into making a peace treaty with them. Now, all he has to do is step back and let these five kings do what should have been done in the first place. God, however, had other plans. Because of this treaty, Joshua and the people of Israel would now have to defend their enemy. What a strange and unexpected twist of events. Israel had given their word, and Joshua understood that a promise made before God is a promise kept, even when it's inconvenient, even when it's undeserved, even when it means defending someone who once stood against you.

When the Gibeonites deceived Israel, the easy response would have been to walk away, to let them face the consequences of their own choices. But God did not let that happen revealing something profound about the heart of God and the weight of covenant. And here is the spiritual truth for us: Faithfulness is not tested in convenience - it is proven in sacrifice. Sometimes God will allow you to be placed in situations where loyalty feels costly, where grace feels heavy, and where obedience requires you to stand with people you would have walked away from in your flesh. But the God you serve is a covenant-keeping God, and He desires that His people reflect the same steadfast nature. Joshua stepped in to defend the Gibeonites not because they earned it, but because Israel had given their word. When you choose character over convenience, when you protect the ones God has assigned to you - even the difficult ones - He will step into your battle and fight alongside you.

The men of Gibeon went to Joshua at Gilgal and said, "Do not forsake your servants; come up to us quickly, save us and help us" (vs. 6). Gilgal is where the base camp of Israel was located. It was the place where Joshua regularly got in God's presence and communicated with Him. Gilgal was more than just Israel's base camp - it was a spiritual landmark, a place where God met His people and where Joshua sought His presence with intentionality and reverence. For Joshua, Gilgal became the consistent meeting place - the place he returned to again and again to hear God's voice, receive divine strategy, and keep his spirit anchored in God's presence. Victory didn't begin on the battlefield; it was birthed in Gilgal. Strength didn't come from numbers or weapons; it flowed from communion with the Lord. We all need a Gilgal, a place where we pause, listen, surrender, and allow God to realign our hearts, a place where the old is rolled away and where clarity comes.

Take notice that Gilgal is mentioned five times in this chapter. This is important because Gilgal in the Old Testament is a picture of Calvary in the New Testament. Gilgal was the place where Israel's new life began when they crossed over the Jordan River. Calvary is where we are given new life in Christ. Gilgal is where God called Israel to erect memorials to always remember what He had done for them. Calvary is where we are called to remember all that Jesus has done for us. Gilgal was the place where they cut away the flesh of their own strength to show their trust in God alone. Calvary is where the strength of our flesh is cut away. Gilgal was the place where Israel first communed with God in the Promised Land. Calvary is what enables our communion with God. Gilgal was the place Joshua first acknowledged God as the Supreme Commander. Calvary is where we first acknowledged Jesus Christ as the Commander of the Lord's Army.

If you want to see God do big things in your life, you must continually remain in His presence. At Gilgal, Joshua lived day after day after day in the presence of God because he knew God's power is found where God is welcomed. His miracles flow where His glory is honored. His breakthroughs come to those who draw near, dwell deep, and stay close. It's not enough to visit God occasionally. Big things happen when you make Him your dwelling place, not your emergency shelter. The presence of God is where faith is strengthened, vision is enlarged, and courage is born. It is where burdens lift, clarity comes, and the impossible becomes possible. When you stay in His presence - through prayer, worship, the Word, and quiet surrender - you position yourself under the open heaven of His favor. You begin to think His thoughts, feel His heartbeat, and move in His strength. Those who stay close to God become witnesses of the extraordinary things only God can do.

At Jericho and Ai, the people of Israel only had one army to fight against. Now there were several armies they must contend with. Joshua had no choice but to go to war for the Gibeonites because of the foolish covenant he made with them. Sometimes in life, we find ourselves bound by decisions we made in moments of weakness, haste, or shortsightedness. Joshua understood this deeply. The covenant he made with the Gibeonites was not born out of wisdom - it was born out of deception, a mistake that could have easily been dismissed, ignored, or justified. But Joshua knew something far greater than convenience: he had given his word before God. When the Gibeonites cried out for help, Joshua had no choice but to go to war on their behalf. Not because they deserved it. Not because it was easy. Not because it was what he wanted. But because integrity demanded it. Covenant demanded it. Obedience to God demanded it.

Fear can come out of regret, but God told Joshua not to be afraid of these kings. He said to Joshua, "Do not fear them, for I have delivered them into your hand; not a man of them shall stand before you" (vs. 8). This upcoming battle was the result of a mistake Joshua made but still God went to war for him. Why? Because Joshua was forever in His presence. He made a mistake but now it was time to move on. Old things have passed away, behold, all things become new (2 Cor. 5:17). Joshua trusted God and immediately went to face the enemy. Vs. 9 says, "Joshua traveled all night from Gilgal and took the Amorite armies by surprise." Why not wait until morning? Joshua knew that if you want to see God do big things, you have to battle for big things. You can't sit back and relax. There's a part you have to play. You have to step into the fight. Joshua understood something that every believer must eventually learn - promised lands are inherited by faith, but they are possessed through battle.

God had already declared victory, but Joshua still had to step forward, sword in hand, trusting that the Lord who promised would also perform. Joshua didn't shrink back when the walls of Jericho towered over him. He didn't retreat when giants filled the land. He didn't doubt when the odds were against him. Instead, he believed that if God called him to it, then God would surely empower him through it. And because Joshua was willing to fight big battles, he saw God release big miracles. Sometimes we want God to move mountains, but we resist climbing them. We pray for breakthrough but avoid the pressure that produces breakthrough. We desire victory but shy away from the fight that leads to victory. Joshua teaches us that faith is not passive - it is active, courageous, and willing to confront whatever stands between us and God's promise. If you want to see God do big things in your life, then don't fear the battle; don't fear the size of the enemy; and don't fear the unknown.

God walks before you so step forward and lift your sword of faith because in the kingdom of God those who battle for big things witness God doing the impossible. When God speaks to you, it's time to fight. Put action to what you believe God will do. Move first. Do something you can do and then God will do something you can't do. In the Kingdom of God, progress often starts with a simple step - a step you can take. God never asks you to do the impossible; He only asks you to move in obedience, faith, and expectation. When you act on what you can do, you make room for God to act on what you cannot do, The Red Sea didn't part until Moses lifted his staff. The walls of Jericho didn't fall until Israel marched. The man with the withered hand wasn't healed until he stretched it out. Peter didn't walk on water until he stepped out of the boat. Each miracle was released after a human step of faith revealing to us that our actions become the invitation for His intervention.

God is waiting for movement so do the part that is within your reach, and you'll see God reach into the part that's beyond your ability. Joshua and his men attached the enemy and "killed them with a great slaughter at Gibeon" (vs. 10). They went to war first, and then God stepped in and did His part. As the enemy fled, the Lord "cast down large hailstones from heaven that continued until they reached Azekah. There were more who died from the hailstones than those who the children of Israel killed with the sword" (vs. 11). In all spiritual battles, you must have your armor on and your boots on the ground. When you do that, God will step in and bring victory from heaven on your behalf. The people fought against the enemy and so did God. They were fighting together. Notice the hailstones fell after Joshua and his men went to war, not before. Why? Because faith without works is dead (James 2:17). The people of Israel had to do something first before God moved.

God always responds when He sees your faith in action. That's why conquerors should always be doing something. Faith-filled obedience is the trigger that brings God onto the scene. When God speaks, the miracle is already present, but it becomes visible the moment you step toward it. Heaven moves when your feet move. Power flows when your heart trusts. Victory manifests when your will aligns with His Word. God gets involved when you step out in faith and begin an all-out war against the enemy. When the men of Israel did what they could do, God moved and did what only He could do. When you go into battle, God will step in and do more than you could ever do on your own. God didn't move before their obedience; He moved through it. Your obedience creates the landing strip for God to move in your life. In spiritual warfare, hesitation is a foothold for the enemy. But obedience, even when your knees are trembling, becomes a weapon. Every step you take in obedience pushes darkness back.

Every moment you choose faith over fear invites God to take center stage in your situation. Faith-filled obedience is not about understanding everything, it's about trusting the One who sees everything. The battle was not yet over, and night-time was fast approaching. Joshua prayed to the Lord in front of all the people, saying, "Sun, stand still over Gibeon; And moon over the valley of Aijalon" (vs. 12). That's a big prayer! He's asking for the earth to stop rotating on its axis! Notice that this was a public prayer. He spoke it out in the sight of all Israel. He didn't quietly whisper this prayer but said it in front of everybody. That's bold faith! Why did he pray publicly? Because he knows this bold prayer will build the faith of those with him. He wanted the people to raise the level of their expectation and believe God to do big things. He wanted everybody to know this wasn't a random accident, it was the power of God at work. Praying publicly points people to the source of answered prayer. It points them to God.

Vs. 13 says, "So the sun stood still, and the moon stopped, until the nation took vengeance on their enemies. So the sun stood still in the midst of heaven and did not hasten to go down for about a whole day." In other words, the earth stopped turning for twenty-four hours. A twenty-four-hour day turned into a forty-eight-hour day because one man prayed a big prayer to a big God. Big prayers unleash God's unlimited resources. It multiplies strength, multiplies wisdom, and multiplies favor. What seemed impossible in a single day becomes possible in one prayer-filled, faith-driven encounter with the Almighty. Vs. 14, "There has never been a day like this one before or since, when the Lord answered such a prayer. Surely the Lord fought for Israel that day!" When you look back over your life and see the mountains He moved, the doors He opened, and the battles He won for you, it becomes undeniable that God is able to do exceedingly, abundantly above all you could ever ask or think (Eph. 3:20).

It is astounding what God did! This story teaches us that bold answers begin with bold prayers. To pray bold prayers, you've got to believe God can do it and will do it. Nothing is too hard for Him. What looks impossible to you is simple to Him. He spoke galaxies into existence and for sure your situation is not beyond His reach. Faith is not just believing in God's power; it's trusting in His willingness. It's knowing that He is good, faithful, and attentive to the cries of His children. When those two truths settle in your spirit, your prayers change. You stop praying timid prayers. You stop asking God for things you think are reasonable. You begin to ask according to His greatness, not your limitations. Conquerors make God happy by asking God for big things. A small prayer is when you ask God for a parking space. A bold prayer is to ask God for a new car that is totally paid for. Ask boldly and God will give boldly! Pray bold prayers with the expectation that God will move on your behalf.

Bold prayers come from a bold confidence in a mighty God. So lift your faith. Stretch your expectations. Ask big, believe big, and watch God move in astounding ways again. Joshua wasn't afraid to pray a bold prayer, and neither should you. When he faced the walls of Jericho, he didn't hesitate, he didn't shrink back, and he didn't rely on his own strength. He trusted God's power and boldly asked for the impossible. And God honored his courage. You, too, are called to pray without fear. Bold prayers don't come from arrogance - they come from faith. When you lift your voice, asking God for breakthrough, wisdom, or favor, do it with confidence, knowing He is able to do far beyond what you can imagine. Don't settle for timid, quiet prayers when God is inviting you to step out in faith. Like Joshua, dare to pray boldly, believe boldly, and act boldly. God's walls are not too high, His plans are not too big, and His power is not too limited. Pray boldly and watch God move in ways only He can.

Bold prayers have to move beyond the realm of what you can see into the realm of what you cannot see. It's in the unseen realm where God does big things. This bold prayer was honored. God did what Joshua asked. Bold prayers honor God so much so that He is ready and willing to give you what you ask. Bold prayers reflect faith, trust, and a recognition of God's power and goodness. They honor Him because they show that we truly believe He can and will act on our behalf. God delights in the courage of a heart that dares to ask, not with hesitation or doubt, but with expectancy. God will go to the extreme to meet the needs of His people, even to the point of making the sun and moon stand still in the sky. There is no limit to what God will do for you if you only believe that He can and will do it. There is no extreme that God will not go to work supernaturally in your life. Boldly approach God and ask Him for big things. Then step back and watch Him move.

| 18 |

"PRAYER WARRIOR"

Every conqueror in God's kingdom is called to a higher purpose - a purpose beyond victories, battles, or personal achievement. The true destiny of a conqueror is not measured by what is won, but by what is released. Let it be known that the destiny of every conqueror is to release the power of God on the earth through prayer. Prayer is the conduit through which God's power flows from heaven to earth. It is in the quiet surrender, the fervent intercession, and the unwavering faith of the conqueror that the miraculous is birthed. Every word spoken in prayer, every act of faith, and every moment of seeking God releases His authority, His favor, and His power into the world. To conquer is not merely to overcome; it is to step into the sacred role of a vessel through which heaven touches earth. Your victories, your perseverance, and your spiritual authority are all designed to unlock the power of God for others, to bring transformation, healing, and divine order wherever you step.

Pray without ceasing. Speak with authority. Release the power of God, and watch as your destiny unfolds in ways that extend far beyond yourself, touching lives, nations, and generations. For sure, prayer is powerful. It changes things. It moves the hand of God. Powerful prayer is the avenue through which needs get met, questions get answered, and lives get changed. James 5:16 says, "The effective, fervent prayer of a righteous man avails much." Effective prayers are prayers that get results. They're prayers God responds to. Joshua prayed and the sun and moon stood still (Josh. 10:13). Prayer saved Daniel in the lion's den (Dan. 6:11). The barren Hannah's steadfast and humble prayers resulted in the prophet Samuel being born (1 Sam. 1:20). Paul's prayer even caused the earth to shake (Acts 16:25,26). How amazing it is that your words can bring God on the scene at any given moment. The fact that prayer can be effective should have you running to your prayer closet as fast as you can go.

Prayer is the doorway into the presence of God. It brings God's kingdom to the earth and is a powerful force in the life of a conqueror. Prayer is not just a ritual; it is the doorway into the very presence of God. When you pray, you step beyond the limitations of the natural and enter into the realm of the divine. It is in this sacred space that God's power flows, His wisdom speaks, and His kingdom manifests on the earth. For the life of a conqueror, prayer is more than a habit - it is a weapon, a shield, and a source of authority. Through prayer, battles are won before they are fought, doors are opened before we even reach them, and victories are secured in alignment with God's will. Every prayer carries the potential to bring heaven to earth. It shifts circumstances, strengthens the spirit, and ignites faith. Let prayer be your first step, your constant companion, and your greatest strategy. For in prayer, the earth trembles under the weight of heaven's presence, and every barrier falls before the God who answers.

A conqueror who prays consistently does not rely on strength alone but operates under the guidance and favor of Almighty God. By praying you partner with God to change the world by releasing His power and resources into the earthly realm. Courageous prayer is believing God can do exceedingly abundantly above all that you can ask or think (Eph. 3:20). It's believing there is no obstacle too big to stop the will of God from being fulfilled on the earth. It is trusting that no matter the obstacle, no matter how insurmountable it may seem, God's will cannot be hindered. Joshua believed this because he prayed for the sun and moon to stand still in the sky. The good news is God designed prayer to get results every time you pray. Jesus promised in John 14:13,14, "And whatever you ask in My name, that I will do, that the Father may be glorified in the Son. If you ask anything in My name, I will do it." How many people pray as if this were true? Based on the condition of their lives, probably not many.

Prayer is more than words; it is the act of believing. When we pray in faith, we align our hearts with heaven's purpose, declaring that mountains may rise, storms may rage, but God's plan will not be stopped. Prayer is the declaration that divine possibilities are greater than human impossibilities. It is the unwavering belief that the power of God is greater than any challenge we face, and that His will is unstoppable on the earth. Let every prayer you lift be a statement of faith: that no barrier, no delay, no opposition can stand against the fulfillment of God's perfect purpose. 1 Peter 3:12, "For the eyes of the Lord are on the righteous, and His ears are open to their prayers." Think about that. When you pray in faith, you've got God's full attention. There is great comfort in knowing that the God who formed the heavens and the earth watches over those who walk with Him. His eyes are not distant, indifferent, or distracted. They are fixed, attentive, loving, and full of purpose.

When the Scripture says His eyes are on the righteous, it means you are never unseen, never forgotten, and never lost in the crowd. God watches over you with the care of a Father and the protection of a King. This verse reminds us that living righteously is not in vain. It positions us under the attentive gaze of God and opens a direct line to His heart. Jesus said in Luke 12:32, "Do not fear, little flock, for it is your Father's good pleasure to give you the kingdom." It makes God happy to do big things for you. He takes pleasure when you pray big prayers. God likes it when you ask the sea to part and the sun to stand still. God will stop the whole universe when somebody prays a big prayer in faith. For most people, their problem is their prayers are too small. They don't pray big prayers to a big God. Stop praying small prayers! The impossible doesn't intimidate God. God isn't offended when you pray big prayers, He's offended when you don't.

Too often we come before the Lord with cautious requests, as if we're afraid to ask for too much. We pray small because we think small all the while forgetting that the One we pray to spoke the universe into existence. The God who parts seas, raises the dead, heals the broken, and turns the hearts of kings is not overwhelmed by what overwhelms us. Your battle is not too hard for the God who specializes in the impossible. Heaven never looks at your prayer and says, "That's too much." The only limit is the one we place on our own faith. So lift your eyes and stretch your faith. Pray prayers that match the size of your God and not the size of your fear. Don't come to the throne of grace with timid requests. Come boldly, confidently, and expectantly, knowing that your Father delights in showing Himself strong on your behalf. When you pray big, you honor God. When you expect miracles, you create room for Him to move. When you believe for the impossible, you position yourself to see His glory.

Stop praying small prayers. Your God is limitless so ask boldly and watch Him do what only He can do. You need to understand that there is tremendous power available to every person in God's kingdom. That power is prayer power. It's power that can move mountains out of the way, close the mouth of lions, and make the sun stand still. Prayer is the key to seeing God do the supernatural in your life. Unless you pray, nothing good will ever happen. Prayer to God should be made persistently (Luke 18:1), with thanksgiving (Phil. 4:6), and in faith (James 2:5). You need to pray within the will of God (Matt. 6:10), for the glory of God (John 14:13,14), and from a heart that is right with God (James 5:16). We serve a big God. He's waiting for you to call on Him to be the big God that He is. God is bigger than your prayers, bigger than your dreams, and bigger than your doubts and fears. God is looking for people who aren't afraid to ask for big things, people with big dreams and visions.

When you go to God, He's always going to ask you what you want. Don't ask for small things. Be bold and tell Him what big thing you want Him to do in your life. There comes a moment in your walk with God when you must stop approaching Him with timid, minimized prayers. God is not intimidated by the size of your request - He is only limited by the size of your expectation. He is the God who spoke galaxies into existence, carved mountains with His words, and breathed life into dust. Nothing you ask can overwhelm Him. God never criticized anyone in Scripture for believing too big - only for believing too small. Blind Bartimaeus asked for sight, not a better begging bowl. The woman with the issue of blood reached for healing, not a little relief. Joshua asked God to make the sun stand still and God did it. The Lord is inviting you to pray prayers that match His power, not your limitations. So lift your eyes. Enlarge your faith. Stretch your expectation.

Tell God the big thing you want Him to do in your life. Ask for the breakthrough that seems impossible. Ask for the healing that doctors can't explain. Ask for the open door that no man can shut. Ask for the restoration, the promotion, the miracle, the destiny-sized blessing. You're not bothering God with big requests - you're honoring Him. Because when you dare to pray big prayers, you give God room to show you just how big He truly is. Pray with boldness because bold prayers honor

God and God honors bold prayers. Prov. 15:8 says, "The prayer of the upright pleases Him." The bolder you pray, the more pleased God is. God is ready to act if you'll be bold enough to ask. He'll bless anyone who is willing to be bold. Jer. 33:3 says, "Call to Me, and I will answer you, and show you great and mighty things." Don't miss the fulfillment of your destiny by asking for small things. Boldly draw near to God and He will boldly draw near to you.

Your faith is released when you pray bold prayers. It's what allows God to do great things in your life and through your life. Your faith is released when you pray bold prayers. Heaven moves when God hears courage in your voice. Bold faith is not reckless, but it is rooted in relationship. It says, "Lord, I believe You are able, and I trust You to do what only You can do. I trust Your heart, even when I can't trace Your hand. I will step forward, believing You will meet me there." Bold faith is the key that unlocks the supernatural. It's the kind of faith opens the door for divine intervention. It invites God to step into your situation with power, wisdom, and favor. When you dare to believe God beyond what your eyes can see, you invite Him to step directly into your situation with power, wisdom, and favor. Bold faith is not loud faith - it is confident faith. It is the quiet assurance that God is who He says He is and will do what He promised, even when circumstances argue otherwise.

Move forward with courage knowing that bold faith opens doors that fear keeps closed and that God is ready to walk through those doors with you. You need to realize that small prayers maintain your life; bold prayers transform your life. When you dare to ask big, you give God room to show Himself strong. Bold faith draws from a bold God. And when you pray with that confidence, He not only does great things for you - He does great things through you. Remember this, your prayers prophecy your future. Your future is founded on the things you pray for. It's big, bold prayers that propel you into your destiny. It's what thrusts you farther ahead than you could ever imagine. There comes a time in every believer's life when ordinary prayers are no longer enough. God is calling you to pray big, to ask boldly, and to believe courageously. Why? Because small prayers may comfort you but big prayers change you. They expand your vision and position you for the destiny God already prepared.

When you pray boldly, you are declaring, "God, I believe You are able. I believe You are willing. And I believe You are leading me into something greater than I can see." Bold prayers unlock doors that fear tries to keep closed. They stir up heaven's attention. They activate God's promises and align your life with His supernatural purpose. Don't be afraid to ask God for things that seem beyond your reach. If it's bigger than you, that means it's just right for Him. God doesn't respond to timidity - He responds to faith. And faith dares to speak what it has not yet seen. Pray prayers that match the greatness of your God. Ask for breakthroughs. Ask for healing. Ask for restoration. Ask for opportunities that only God can orchestrate. Ask for the impossible. Because it's big, bold prayers that propel you into your destiny and your destiny is waiting for you to rise up and believe. Heaven waits for the sound of your voice. God is not intimidated by the size of your need - He is honored by the size of your faith.

You are only one bold prayer away from a miracle. One moment of courage, one act of trust, one cry of the heart that says, "Lord, I believe You can do what no one else can." Don't settle for small requests when you serve a limitless God. Call on Him for great things. Ask big. Believe boldly. Pray with expectation. The same God who parted seas, raised the dead, and opened prison doors is the God who hears you now. Dare to pray beyond what seems possible. Your miracle may be closer than you think. In fact, it's just one bold prayer away. Paul was a prayer warrior. What motivated him to pray with such boldness? Speaking of Jesus, Paul said in Eph. 3:12, "In Whom we have boldness and access with confidence through our faith in Him." You can pray bold, powerful prayers because you are God's child. You've been bought and paid for by the blood of Christ. You don't go to God as a stranger but as an heir to the promise.

You can approach God boldly and with confidence to seek whatever it is you need from Him. You can do this because you are a conqueror in whom the Spirit of God dwells. Rom. 8:37 says, "In all things we are more than conquerors through Him who loved us." Paul said in Christ you have boldness, access, and confidence. These are the three main ingredients of a powerful prayer. The Greek word for "boldness" means 'freedom of speech.' When you're bold, you can speak what's on your mind. It's an openness that stems from freedom and a lack of fear. With boldness you go to God without apprehension because you're not afraid He'll reject you. Heb. 4:16 (AMP), "Let us then fearlessly and confidently and boldly draw near to the throne of grace." God loves it when you do that. When you're bold you can continually approach God without fear and without reservation. The Message Bible says, "So let's walk right up to Him and get what He is ready to give. Take the mercy, accept the help."

The word "access" literally means 'a bringing near.' The moment you get saved, Jesus introduced you to the Father. He gave you access to Him. What was unthinkable to the Old Testament Jew is now available to all who come to Christ by grace through faith. Through Christ you can go to the Father with boldness knowing you'll be welcomed with opened arms. The blood of Jesus gives you freedom of entry and access to the throne room of God. Because of Christ's sacrifice, you are no longer an outsider looking in. The veil that once separated humanity from God's holy presence has been torn from top to bottom. You don't come trembling through a doorway of judgment - you come boldly through a doorway of grace. When the Father looks at you, He does not see your past failures or your weaknesses. He sees the blood of His Son covering you, cleansing you, and declaring you righteous. The blood of Jesus is your passport into the presence of the Almighty.

The power that flowed out of Jesus was connected to the access He had with the Father through prayer. A lot of people don't ask God for big things because they're not connected to Him. They're looking at their big problems and have no confidence in the sovereign God of the universe. Heaven's throne room is not a place of dread for you - it is your home, your refuge, and the place where your Father waits with open arms. Come freely. Come boldly. Come often. Access is the freedom conquerors possess to speak to God in prayer anytime, anywhere. Prayer gives you access to heaven and the power to control what happens on the earth (Matt. 16:19). Heaven responds when you pray. Angels move when you pray. Doors shift when you pray. Circumstances change when you pray. Prayer is not passive - it is powerful. It is the spiritual bridge that connects God's will in heaven with God's work on earth. Prayer gives you access. Prayer gives you authority. Prayer changes everything.

Don't speak as though you're powerless. Enter heaven's throne room boldly and let heaven invade earth through the words you speak in faith. When you pray, you begin with boldness and end with confidence. Praying boldly shows you have confidence in the authority of Jesus over everything the enemy brings against you. Confidence is the assurance of a ready welcome and loving response which is all possible through faith in the Lord Jesus Christ. The word means "full persuasion" and expresses a belief in someone to the point of placing one's trust and reliance in them. It's really not prayer unless you have confidence in Who you're praying to and what you're praying about. Confidence gives you the assurance that when you pray, God hears you. 1 John 5:14,15 says, "And we are confident that He hears us whenever we ask for anything that pleases Him. And since we know he hears us when we make our requests, we also know that He will give us what we ask for."

| 19 |

"CLOSE THE GAP"

Your own personal Promised Land was designed by God to be a land of continual blessing. Long before you took your first breath, God crafted a place of blessing uniquely suited for you. It isn't a random territory or a mere dream you happen to desire. It is your Promised Land - prepared, appointed, and anointed by God Himself. In that land, blessing isn't occasional. It is continual. It flows like a river, not a raindrop. Just as the children of Israel entered a land flowing with milk and honey, God has a place for you flowing with purpose, peace, provision, and His unshakable presence. The blessings there don't depend on the world's economy, the opinions of people, or the instability of circumstances. They rest on the faithfulness of the One who promised. Your personal promised land was designed by God to be a land of continual blessing and nothing can stop what God has already prepared for you. Just remember that every promised land requires faith. You must believe that what God said is already yours.

The blessings are there but you must be willing to step into it even when giants appear and walls seem high. Sad to say, a lot of people experience these blessings once in a while but not all the time. For them, it's hit-and-miss. A blessing here, a blessing there with a whole lot of hardship in between. This is not how God designed your life to be. In fact, it's the exact opposite. You're supposed to be blessed all the time, with a little hardship here and a little hardship there. Lam. 3:22,23 says, "His compassions fail not. They are new every morning; Great is Your faithfulness." Every morning God has a new blessing waiting for you. Of course, these blessings are not automatic. There are some things you must do to get them. To experience the blessings of your Promised Land, you must be wholehearted, fully devoted to God. When you're wholehearted, you hold nothing back. You give God all of you choosing, in every moment, to offer your heart, your thoughts, your actions, and your desires to Him.

God desires more than just a portion of your heart. He longs for all of you. The word "wholehearted" carries a depth of meaning that touches the very core of your spiritual life. It means to be completely and sincerely devoted, determined, enthusiastic, and energetic in everything you do for God. It means offering not just a part of your heart, but your entire being - your thoughts, your actions, and your passions to His service. A wholehearted life is not half-hearted in faith, not lukewarm in love, and not distracted by the temporary things of this world. It is a life fully surrendered, fully alive, and fully committed to walking in God's ways, free from all reserve and hesitation. As the Scripture says, "You shall love the Lord your

God with all your heart, and with all your soul, and with all your strength" (Deut. 6:5). When you serve God wholeheartedly, your devotion becomes a living testimony, your determination becomes a beacon, and your energy and enthusiasm inspire others to seek His presence.

To truly serve God, you must offer every corner of your life, surrendering your will and your ways to His divine guidance. When you lay down your plans and ambitions, giving God your complete devotion, your life becomes a living sacrifice, pleasing in His sight. True faith is not partial - it is total, a full commitment where every heartbeat, every decision, and every desire is offered in love and obedience. Caleb stands out as a powerful example of unwavering faith and courage. In Scripture, six times it is recorded that he "wholly followed the Lord God of Israel" (Num. 14:24, 32:12; Deut. 1:36; Josh. 14:8,9,14). Doing this is the most important thing a conqueror can do in order to take full possession of the Promised Land. This wasn't a half-hearted commitment; it was a life fully surrendered, a heart entirely devoted. Because of this, Caleb had the heart of a conqueror - undaunted by giants, unshaken by fear, and unmovable in the face of obstacles.

The secret of Caleb's victory wasn't in his strength or strategies - it was in his steadfast devotion to God. He saw possibilities where others saw impossibilities because his heart was aligned with the Almighty. When you, like Caleb, wholly follow God, trusting Him in every challenge and holding firm to His promises, you also will inherit a conqueror's heart. Caleb's example reminds us that true conquest begins in the heart. Faithful obedience, unwavering courage, and a life wholly surrendered to God empower us to overcome every giant in our path. God honors the heart that follows Him fully. God said in Num. 14:24, "But because my servant Caleb has a different spirit and follows Me wholeheartedly, I will bring him into the land he went to, and his descendants will inherit it." The term "follows Me wholeheartedly" is a hunting term. It means to 'close the gap' like a hunter who closes in on his prey. Caleb closed the gap between him and God. He pursued God, he went after Him.

All his life, Caleb refused to let anything come between him and God. He didn't wait for the distance to close on its own - he took the steps to close the gap himself. Every choice, every moment, every act of obedience brought him closer. This is what it means to be wholehearted: not merely following from afar, but walking close, leaning in, and surrendering fully. True devotion isn't passive; it's an active pursuit of God's presence, a life that says, "I will not be content with anything less than all of You." Caleb's heart was undivided, and in that undivided heart, he found God's fullness. Say, "God, I want to be as close to You as I possibly can be. I am going to pursue You with everything that is within me." You can't be a conqueror and not follow the Lord. When you're wholehearted, you follow Jesus without hesitation or reservation. Jesus said in John 10:27, "My sheep hear My voice, and I know them, and they follow Me."

Eighteen times in the gospels Jesus simply and powerfully said, "Follow Me." On the surface, it seems straightforward - a call to obedience, a request to come after Him. But in the original Greek language the word "follow" carries a deeper, richer meaning. It means 'to walk the same road.' It's not just about believing in Him or admiring Him from a distance. It's about joining Him on the journey, step by step, day by day. Following the Lord is to be a habitual, moment-by-moment continuance. To follow Jesus is to take His path, embrace His priorities, carry His values, and allow His Spirit to guide your pace. It's walking where He walks, thinking how He thinks, and loving how He loves. Following Jesus may not always be easy for the road is narrow, the path may wind through trials, and the crowd may go another way. Still, the invitation is steadfast: walk with Me. Every step you take with Him transforms your heart, reshapes your mind, and draws you closer into the life He came to give.

Caleb is an example to all conquerors on how to face challenges with confidence, strength, joy, and gladness. He had a zeal for life! He was excited about the future! He was raring to go! He was a man whose heart was full of faith! Caleb goes to Joshua and boldly proclaims, "I wholly followed the Lord my God" (Josh. 14:8). He then said in vs. 12, "Now therefore, give me this mountain that the Lord promised me." When you live with a wholehearted heart, fully surrendered and trusting in God, faith becomes your key to claiming the blessings and promises that belong to you. Half-hearted efforts and doubt will only delay your inheritance, but a heart fully devoted, aligned with His will, moves mountains. Step forward boldly, speak in faith, and act with confidence, knowing that what God has set aside for you cannot be withheld. Your faith isn't just a feeling - it's the bridge between your obedience and your destiny. Take hold of it, for what belongs to you is already within reach.

There are incredible blessings reserved for those who close the gap between themselves and God. When you draw near, setting aside distractions, pride, and fear, His presence fills the spaces in your hearts that you didn't even know were empty. Peace replaces anxiety, clarity replaces confusion, and purpose replaces aimlessness. Doors that once seemed locked swing open, guidance becomes unmistakable, and favor flows in ways that cannot be explained by human effort alone. The journey toward God is not always easy, but every step taken in faith narrows the distance, and every step brings the promise of His abundant blessings. Being wholehearted adds power to your faith. It will help you believe His promises. If you believe, you'll receive. If you don't, you won't. It's as simple as that. Vs. 13,14 says, "And Joshua blessed him, and gave Hebron to Caleb as an inheritance. Hebron therefore became the inheritance of Caleb because he wholly followed the Lord God of Israel."

Caleb didn't ask for the easy, lush pasture lands of the valley. He didn't chase comfort, security, or the path that everyone else was taking. While others were content with what was safe and plentiful, Caleb set his eyes on Hebron - a land that was tougher to take, more challenging to possess, yet promised greater reward. Hebron was located on the top of a rugged mountain range. Hebron was the powerful stronghold for a race of giants who lived in great fortified cities. Why Hebron? Why seek such a difficult place for your inheritance? It was at Hebron where God came down and spoke to Abraham face-to-face. Hebron was where God made a relationship with Him possible. The word "Hebron" means 'to keep company, to be associated with.' It carries the idea of fellowship, communion, and friendship, as in being a friend of God. Hebron was not just a city; it was a promise. Caleb said, "All I want is Hebron." He wanted to close the gap no matter the cost, no matter the difficulty.

Spiritually, this teaches us that God often calls His people to more than what is easy. Faith, courage, and persistence are required to claim the inheritance He has prepared for us. The abundant valleys of life may feel safe and appealing, but Hebron represents purpose, destiny, and fulfillment - the places God calls you to that demand your trust and your boldness. Caleb's choice reminds us that true victory comes not from avoiding difficulty, but from pursuing God's best, even when it requires stepping into the unknown, facing giants, and refusing to settle for less than what God has destined for us. Caleb was bold, strong, faithful, and wholehearted. He followed the Lord fully and he's bold in faith. He's ready to face the giants at Hebron with confidence. He said in Josh. 14:12, "It may be that the Lord will be with me, and I shall be able to drive them out as the Lord said." We learn from Caleb that being wholehearted builds your faith. Being wholehearted will propel you into believing God for big things in your life.

Faith doesn't come automatically; fear and doubt does. The mind trembles at uncertainty, the heart worries at the unknown. You don't have to try to doubt, it just happens. It comes uninvited, quietly or loudly, as a part of being human.

Faith, on the other hand, is not accidental. It is deliberate. It is a chosen lifestyle that is cultivated by closing the gap, by getting close to God. It is nurtured through prayer, study, reflection, and trust in God's promises. The closer you are to God, the easier it will be to believe His Word and for His power to work in your life. While doubt may arise naturally, faith grows intentionally. Every act of obedience, every moment of gratitude, every step taken in trust is like water on the soil of your soul, helping faith take root and flourish. Remember: you cannot prevent doubt, but you can strengthen faith. Let your focus be on tending the garden of your spirit, and faith will blossom even in the presence of uncertainty.

Faith rises when you refuse to let fear dictate your steps, when you speak truth over the lies of doubt, and when you trust God even when circumstances scream otherwise. Faith requires effort, patience, and persistence. It is cultivated by obedience, nourished by God's Word, and strengthened in prayer. And the beautiful truth is the more you exercise faith, the more fear loses its grip. Doubt fades. What once seemed impossible becomes a testimony. Don't wait until a crisis comes to build your faith. Faith is not meant to be a last resort; it is meant to be a foundation. Too often, we wait until life shakes us to our core before we turn to God. But faith built in the calm, nurtured daily through prayer, scripture, and obedience, stands strong when the storms come. Faith is cultivated over time, not suddenly summoned in panic. Don't wait for a crisis to realize you need God. Build your relationship with Him today and be ready to stand firm tomorrow.

It's better to build your faith before you need your faith. If you wait until the waves crash and the winds roar, your faith may be tested to the point of breaking. Start now. Strengthen your trust in God in the ordinary moments, in the quiet seasons, and in the small decisions. When the unexpected trials arrive, you will not be overwhelmed - you will be anchored, unshaken, and able to walk through challenges with confidence, knowing God is your refuge and strength. You can't build mountain-moving faith in a moment's notice. It must be cultivated. Invest time in prayer, in the study of God's Word, and nurture a relationship with Him now, when life feels easy. Strengthen your trust in God daily, so when challenges arise - unexpected trials, loss, or uncertainty - your faith won't waver. A prepared heart is a resilient heart. Remember, faith built in advance carries you through the darkest nights. Don't wait for the storm to come; start building your faith today.

Caleb built up his faith forty years before he needed it. Forty years earlier he said to Moses, "Let us go up at once and take possession, for we are well able to overcome it" (Num. 13:30). This declaration is more than courage - it is a profound statement of faith. He was not merely assessing the size of the enemy or the strength of the land. He was trusting in God's promise and power. Caleb saw beyond the giants and the fortified cities; he saw God's faithfulness. His confidence was rooted not in his own strength, but in the assurance that God equips those who obey Him to conquer what seems impossible. This moment reminds us that faith calls for action. Belief is not passive, it moves forward. Like Caleb, we are often called to step into situations that seem overwhelming, but with God, we are well able to overcome. Let Caleb's words stir courage in your heart. Move forward with faith trusting God to go before you knowing that His power makes you more than able to take the land.

Caleb was a man who walked by faith and not by sight (2 Cor. 5:7). Faith is more than belief - it is the lens through which we perceive life. What you see and how you see it is shaped by the depth of your faith. When your faith is strong, ordinary moments become extraordinary, challenges transform into opportunities, and the unseen hand of God becomes visible in every circumstance. Faith allows you to see as God sees. It opens your eyes to His purposes, His timing, and His provision. Where doubt sees obstacles, faith sees doors. Where fear sees failure, faith sees victory. When your vision aligns with God's, you begin to recognize blessings in disguise, lessons in hardship, and His infinite love in every detail of your journey. Hold fast to faith, for it is the lens that turns the world from gray into divine light. Through faith, your eyes are opened to see not just the world around you, but the Kingdom within it. What should you do? The same thing Caleb did. Close the gap and when you need faith, it will be there.

Caleb was one of the twelve men sent by Moses to spy out the Promised Land. Ten spies brought back an evil report because they feared the giants who were there. They said they were like grasshoppers compared to the giants in the Promised Land (Num. 13:33). But Caleb had a different spirit about him. He had the heart of a conqueror. He quieted the people and said, "Let us go up at once and take possession, for we are well able to take the land" (Num. 13:30). Caleb had this confidence in God because he was wholehearted in his commitment to Him. Caleb said in Num. 14:9, "Their protection is gone, but the Lord is with us. Do not be afraid of them." Faith gives you convictions no one else has. He's saying, "If God be for us, who can be against us?" (Rom. 8:31). How does Caleb know the Lord is with them? When you close the gap, you know where God is. Caleb was wholehearted and he knows God is right beside him. "Draw near to God and He will draw near to you" (James 4:8).

Caleb is eighty-five and he said, "Yet I am as strong this day as I was in the day that Moses sent me; just as my strength was then, so now is my strength for war" (vs. 11). Can you really be strong in your old age? God gave Caleb a promise and gave him strength at eighty-five to defeat the giants at Hebron. Never think you're too old to take possession of your Promised Land. At eighty-five Caleb didn't want to sit back and fish all day. No, he wanted to go fight giants. You can retire from your job, but you never retire from serving the Lord. This is why Caleb said, "Give me this mountain!" (vs. 12). Clint Eastwood told how he was still being productive and making movies as he neared the end of his life. He said, "I just get up every morning and go out and I don't let the old man in." Caleb defeated the giants and took his mountain because he didn't let the old man in. Never think you're too old to be productive in the kingdom of God. Your best days are ahead of you if you don't let the old man in.

| 20 |

"TRUE COMMITMENT"

The book of Joshua stands as a powerful reminder that walking with God requires strength, courage, and unwavering devotion. When the Lord called Joshua to lead His people into the Promised Land, He didn't simply give him a task - He gave him a promise saying, "I will be with you wherever you go." That same promise still carries strength for us today. Joshua teaches us that true courage is not the absence of fear, but the willingness to step forward in obedience even when the path is uncertain. It is the boldness that comes from knowing God goes ahead of us, walks beside us, and strengthens us from within. But Joshua also teaches us something just as important: obedience is the key to victory. God instructed His people to meditate on His Word day and night and to follow all that He commanded. When they obeyed, walls fell, rivers parted, and enemies scattered. When they turned aside, they stumbled.

In our lives, idols still try to compete for our hearts - comfort, fear, pride, possessions, people, and even our own plans. The message of Joshua calls us to turn away from every idol and renew our devotion to the Lord alone. When we stand firm in faith, walk in obedience, and commit our whole heart to God, we will see His faithfulness just as Joshua did. He still leads. He still speaks. And He still calls us to be strong and courageous, for the battle belongs to Him. And now, in the final chapter of Joshua, it is time to choose whom we will serve. Joshua is advanced in age and before he dies he gives a farewell address to the people of Israel. Joshua 24 begins with Joshua reviewing all the great and glorious acts of God. He then calls upon the people to show gratitude for all the Lord has done. Based on the incredible outpouring of divine grace on the people of Israel, Joshua now stands before the people and speaks with boldness and clarity.

He said in vs. 14,15, "Now therefore, fear the Lord, serve Him in sincerity and in truth. Throw away the gods your forefathers worshipped beyond the River and in Egypt and serve the Lord. Choose for yourselves this day whom you will serve. As for me and my house, we will serve the Lord." Joshua stood before the people of Israel at a defining moment. After years of victories, battles, miracles, and the faithfulness of God on full display, he brought the nation to a place of decision. He wasn't speaking as a young warrior anymore, but as a seasoned servant of the Lord as one who had seen firsthand that God keeps every promise He makes. He didn't ask the people to do anything he wasn't already living. He modeled devotion. He set the standard. He publicly aligned his life, his household, and his future with the purposes of God. Joshua made a commitment to the Lord before the people and he's asking them to do the same thing.

Not only do you live out your devotions, you're also to declare your devotion. It matters that the world knows who you belong to. It matters that your voice aligns with your heart. Vocalize your commitment to God. Be like Joshua and boldly declare that God is whom you will serve. When you openly declare your devotion to God, you're not just making a statement, you're making a stand. You're saying, "I am His, and He is mine." You're affirming your commitment not only before heaven, but before people, circumstances, and even the enemy who tests your resolve. God is honored when His children are unashamed to identify with Him. Jesus said in Matt. 10:32,33 says "Whoever confesses Me before men, him I will also confess before My Father who is in heaven. But whoever denies Me before men, him I will also deny before My Father who is in heaven." There is a blessing attached to a bold confession. Let your life reflect your devotion and let your mouth confirm it.

Some people declare they're devoted to God but don't live like it. They talk better than they live. Matt. 15:8, "These people draw near to me with their mouth, and honor Me with their lips but their heart is far from Me." God is not impressed by words alone. He is not moved by rehearsed phrases, religious expressions, or outward gestures that are empty of love. The Lord searches beyond what the mouth declares and the hands perform and looks straight into the heart. In this scripture, Jesus confronts a tragic truth: it is possible to sound spiritual while being spiritually distant. It is possible to say all the right things yet have a heart that is disengaged, indifferent, or distracted. Lip-service is easy; true devotion costs something. But God is calling His people to more than appearances. He is inviting us into authenticity, into worship that begins in the heart and flows outward. True honor is not spoken first; it is lived first. It shows up in how we love, how we obey, how we trust Him when no one is watching.

God is not condemning us with these words; He is calling us back. He wants a relationship that is heartfelt, humble, and whole. He desires worship that arises from gratitude, repentance, and love - not routine or obligation. For when the heart is right, the words will follow and God will delight in both. What should your response be to the incredible grace and victory and provision that God has poured into your life? Joshua says your only reasonable response to all the Lord has done is to fear the Lord and serve Him. Joshua is making a passionate plea to the people to be totally devoted to God and to have their hearts set on Him. He wants the people to commit to serving the Lord with all faithfulness, integrity, sincerity, and loyalty. The words "Now therefore" indicates that the commitment Joshua is demanding is the logical response to what God has done. He wants them to be wholehearted, to live a life fully aware of who God is and what He expects them to do.

The first thing Joshua commands the people to do is fear the Lord, to have a holy reverence for Him. This does not mean to be afraid of God but to have a wholesome dread of displeasing Him. The fear of the Lord means to love God and hate sin. When you wholeheartedly fear the Lord by reverencing His holiness, honoring His wisdom, and recognizing His authority, you step into a life anchored by divine confidence. The fear of the Lord is not terror; it is trust, awe, and surrender. It is the realization that His ways are higher, His thoughts are perfect, and His guidance is unfailing. When you trust Him fully, you no longer walk by sight alone. You walk by faith - steady, secure, and bold. Confidence rises in your heart because you know the One who leads you cannot fail. His commands become your compass. His promises become your foundation. His presence becomes your strength. As you follow Him, obedience is no longer a burden but a joy.

Joshua then commands the people to serve God in sincerity and in truth. Notice that godly fear leads to godly activity. When you fear the Lord, when you give your heart wholly and completely to Him, you'll be able to serve Him in sincerity and in truth. In Joshua 24, the word "serve" occurs nineteen times. His words focus on an inner attitude and an outer lifestyle. Other translations say to serve Him "completely and sincerely" (NASB), "in righteousness and justice" (LXE), "with all faithfulness" (NIV), "with integrity and loyalty" (NET). Rom. 12:1 says, "By the mercies of God, present your bodies a living sacrifice, holy, acceptable to God, which is your reasonable service." The word "sincerity" means 'without blemish, perfect, integrity.' It means 'to be complete. entire, whole.' It refers to the quality of life characterized by honesty, integrity, justice, righteousness, and uprightness. The word "truth" means 'to confirm, support, believe, be faithful.' It means 'faithfulness, that which gives complete reliability.'

God is faithful (Ps. 91:4) and he is called the "God of truth" (Ps. 31:5). Together the words "sincerity" and 'truth' paint a picture of being without hypocrisy. Sincerity speaks of the heart: pure motives, clean intentions, and a spirit that refuses to wear a mask. Truth speaks of the path: the unwavering standard of God's Word, the light that exposes what is real and strengthens what is right. When sincerity fills the heart and truth guides the walk, a believer becomes whole and undivided. There is no double life, no hidden agenda, no pretending to be something on the outside that is not real on the inside. Instead, there is a quiet strength, a steady integrity, a life that reflects Christ from the inside out. Aim to be a person whose heart is sincere and whose steps are rooted in truth so that what you profess with your lips is seen in the purity of your life. For this is the path that reflects the very nature of Jesus, who is both perfectly sincere and perfectly true.

Serve the Lord with wholeness and blamelessness. Serve Him with perfection, with all that is in you. Serving the Lord implies He is your Master. If the Lord is to be served, all other gods and idols must be removed and put away. This is why Joshua told the people to put away the false gods their fathers served in Egypt. He knew if you give the devil an inch, he'll take a mile. The enemy never asks for much - at least not at first. He only wants a small compromise, a little loosening of conviction, a single moment of "just this once." But what begins as an inch soon becomes a foothold, and a foothold can become a stronghold if left unchecked. This is why he's asking the people to make a total and complete commitment to the Lord. Everything that takes the place of God in your life must be cast away. Many people serve God on Sunday and other gods the rest of the week. They're not wholly committed. They let other things occupy in their life what only God should occupy.

Whatever takes the place of God in your life can be called an idol or a false god. Even good things can become bad if they take the place of God. Idols aren't always carved statues or ancient symbols. Many times they look like everyday blessings: relationships, careers, ambitions, gifts, ministries, or even our own plans. These things are not evil in themselves; in fact, they are often given by God. But when they begin to claim first place in your heart, when they shape your decisions more than God does, when they receive the attention, trust, or devotion that belongs to Him alone they quietly become false gods. An idol is anything we rely on more than God, love more than God, or fear losing more than God. God calls us to enjoy the blessings He gives, but never to replace the Blesser. He invites us to lay everything at His feet, trusting that He alone satisfies, He alone secures, and He alone deserves the throne of our hearts. If He's not first, nothing else will be in its proper place.

When God is first, everything else in life finds divine order, peace, and meaning. Understand that family time is a good thing unless it continually keeps you from going to church. There is danger in turning your family into a false god. Go to church together as a family and then go to the beach. Many people put their job and career above God.

They're so busy trying to make a fortune that they leave God out of their lives. For them, their career has become a false god. Hobbies can also be a false god. Going fishing or playing golf when you should be in church makes an idol out of your hobbies. Physical fitness can be a false god. Some people would rather go to the gym and work out than read their Bible and go to church. Sports and video games can be false gods, as well as money, sex, alcohol, drugs, and food. Stop and think about it. What you do with your time is what you're doing with your life. How much time do you spend with God compared to the time you spend on other things?

Don't let your loyalty to God be divided. You must serve the Lord and Him only. In Matthew 6:24, Jesus draws a clear line in the sand, "No one can serve two masters; for either he will hate the one and love the other, or else he will be loyal to the one and despise the other." These words remind us that the human heart was never designed for divided allegiance. We were created to live with a single devotion, a single truth, a single guiding love. Every day, we stand at a crossroads between the kingdom of God and the pull of this world. The world offers distraction, comfort, and self-reliance. God offers purpose, holiness, and eternal life. But Jesus makes it unmistakably clear - you cannot cling to both. To choose Christ is to release every competing loyalty. It is to declare with your life, "Lord, You alone are my Master." This means trusting Him when it's difficult, obeying Him when it's unpopular, and loving Him above every other voice that seeks your attention.

Joshua knew if the people didn't put away their false gods, they would eventually serve them and not the living God. That's why you have to pay attention to your affections and the things you put in your heart. How do you know if something is an idol to you? Ask yourself, what do you treasure? What do you fear losing? What can't you let go of? In the Parable of the Sower, Jesus said, "The desire for other things entering in choke the word and it becomes unfruitful" (Mark 4:19). That's idolatry! Don't let the things of this world choke God out of your life. Conquerors give God the time and attention and affection He so rightfully deserves. They are not defined by their strength, their victories, or the battles they overcome. They are defined by the posture of their heart toward God. A conqueror is someone who understands that every triumph begins with surrender - not to the enemy, but to the Lord who fights on their behalf.

Conquerors give God their time because they know no time spent with Him is ever wasted. In His presence they receive clarity, courage, and direction. They understand that the battles of life are won privately before victory is ever seen publicly. Conquerors give God their attention because their eyes stay fixed on the One who goes before them. While others are distracted by noise, pressure, and fear, conquerors remain focused on God's voice. They refuse to look at the size of the giants when they can look at the greatness of their God. Conquerors give God their affection because their hearts belong to Him above all else. They know that worship strengthens their spirit, and love for God anchors their soul. Their devotion is not based on circumstances but built on relationship. When you give God what He rightfully deserves, He makes you into what He always intended - a conqueror, more than victorious through Christ who loves you.

The point is this: It's not what you possess that matters, it's what possesses you. Joshua said to the people, "Choose for yourselves this day whom you will serve." Everybody is going to serve something or someone. Everybody! We all have a choice as to who or what we will serve. It's the same choice confronting every person in every age. You either serve the Lord or you don't. Joshua is calling for a commitment from the people. He demanded a decision from them, and rightly so. He called for a commitment - not a casual agreement, but a wholehearted decision. He demanded that they choose whom they would serve, recognizing that neutrality was not an option. In his words, there was urgency, clarity, and a reminder of the consequences of indecision. While this is a command, God will not force you to make the right choice. He always leaves the choice to our will. Will we walk in His way or our own way? His way is the highway of holiness, our way leads to ruin.

While choosing, just remember that God is a jealous God (Josh. 24:19) and He'll share His glory with no one. God seeks only those with a willing heart and mind to serve Him in spirit and in truth. To be a conqueror, you've got to choose God above everything and everyone else. Joshua boldly called for a deep and true commitment to the Lord. To compel them to make the right decision, Joshua declares his own. He says, "But as for me and my house, we will serve the Lord" (vs. 15). A man's personal example is more powerful than words. It is easy to speak about faith, morality, or character, but true influence comes not from what a man says - it comes from how he lives. Every action, every choice, every moment of integrity becomes a silent sermon that others cannot ignore. When a man walks in humility, honesty, and love, his life becomes a testimony that words alone could never convey. The Bible reminds us, "In everything set them an example by doing what is good" (Titus 2:7).

People watch more than they listen. They are inspired not by sermons but by lives that reflect God's light in tangible ways. A life lived faithfully encourages, strengthens, and points others to Christ far more effectively than any speech or teaching. Let your life be a beacon. Let your actions reflect your faith. Speak less, live more, and watch as your personal example opens hearts that words alone cannot reach. Moses told the people what to do once they entered the Promised Land. Deut. 6:2 says they were to "fear the Lord your God, to keep all His statutes and His commandments." Vs. 5 says, "You shall love the Lord your God with all your heart, with all your soul, and with all your might." Declare your devotion to your family, to fellow believers, to your coworkers, to the stranger on the street. Then go out and put action to what you declared. Give those around you an example to follow. Let them see you serving God with wholehearted devotion. Hopefully they will come to serve Him too.

SUMMARY

As we reach the conclusion of "The Heart Of A Conqueror," we are reminded that the journey of Joshua and the children of Israel is far more than a historical account - it is a blueprint for spiritual victory. Their story illustrates that conquering the challenges of life requires more than strength or strategy; it demands faith, obedience, courage, and an unwavering trust in God's promises.

Through the triumphs and trials of the Israelites, we have seen that true conquest begins in the heart. It begins when fear is replaced by faith, doubt is replaced by obedience, and the ordinary is empowered by the extraordinary hand of God. Every battle they faced, every wall that fell, and every step toward the Promised Land teaches us that victory is not merely inherited - it is actively pursued through steadfast faith and bold action.

May the lessons within these pages inspire you to cultivate the heart of a conqueror: a heart that dares to trust God, a heart that rises above fear, and a heart that presses forward toward the promises He has prepared for you. Like Joshua, may you lead your life with courage, claim your spiritual inheritance with confidence, and walk daily in the fullness of God's victory.

The Promised Land awaits those who are willing to step out in faith. Will you walk boldly with the heart of a conqueror?